Effect Oriented Programming

A New Paradigm for Creating Reliable, Adaptable, Testable Systems - Using Scala and ZIO

Bill Frasure, Bruce Eckel, and James Ward

Effect Oriented Programming

A New Paradigm for Creating Reliable, Adaptable, Testable Systems - Using Scala and ZIO

Bill Frasure, Bruce Eckel, and James Ward

ISBN 978-0-9818725-7-5

Leanpub

This is a Leanpub book. Leanpub empowers authors and publishers with the Lean Publishing process. Lean Publishing is the act of publishing an in-progress ebook using lightweight tools and many iterations to get reader feedback, pivot until you have the right book and build traction once you do.

eBook ISBN 978-0-9818725-6-8

Print Book ISBN 978-0-9818725-7-5

The eBook is available through www.EffectOrientedProgramming.com.

Contents

CONTENTS

1: Preface

Effects are the unpredictable parts of a system. Traditional programs are hard to build and maintain because they do not isolate these parts.

Effect Systems partition the unpredictable parts and manage them separately from the predictable ones. With Effect Systems, developers can more easily build applications that are reliable, adaptable, and testable.

Effect Oriented Programming is a new paradigm for programming with Effect Systems.

Since Effect Systems are a new and emerging paradigm, you have limited choices. Many programming languages do not have an Effect System. Some languages have built-in support for managing Effects, while others have support through libraries. New languages that incorporate Effect Systems include OCaml, Unison, and Roc.

In this book, we focus on the concepts of Effect Systems, rather than language and library specifics.

1.1: Scala 3 & ZIO

We use Scala 3, which has several Effect System libraries including ZIO, Cats Effects, and Kyo. These libraries (and others) contributed to our understanding of Effect Systems. We chose the ZIO library for this book because of both our satisfaction with it and our experience—one author (Bill) was an engineer at Ziverge, the company that created and maintains ZIO, for several years.

This is not a book about ZIO. You do not need experience or understanding of ZIO to understand the code in this book. For this book, ZIO is only a means to understand Effect Systems.

If you use a different language, the concepts of Effect Systems may only be useful when your language or a library supports them. However, learning the concepts presented here will prepare you.

While in-depth Scala knowledge is not required to learn the concepts, this book assumes you are familiar with:

- Functions
- Strong static typing
- Chaining operations on objects, as in:

```
"asdf ".trim.length
```

To learn more about ZIO, consult their documentation[1].

1.2: Code Examples

The book's examples are available on GitHub[2].

This book uses Scala 3 language syntax that might be unfamiliar, even to Scala developers. Our focus is on the concepts of Effect Oriented Programming, so we've made the examples very readable, even on mobile devices. To achieve this, we optimize syntax to constrain the width of our listings. For

---

[1]https://effectorientedprogramming.com/resources/zio/docs
[2]https://effectorientedprogramming.com/resources/zio/examples/2024-09-17

example, we often use Scala 3's *significant indentation* with single-parameter functions. The function name is followed by a colon (:), and the single argument is indented on the following line:

```
ZIO.debug:
  "hello, world"
```

`ZIO.debug` displays its argument on the console. The traditional approach, using parentheses, looks like this:

```
ZIO.debug("hello, world")
```

Significant indentation only works for single-parameter functions. For multi-parameter functions and in cases where the single argument is brief and does not contain nested function calls, we use traditional syntax:

```
ZIO.debug("cat", "dog", "bird")
```

```
ZIO.debug(1)
```

1.2.1: Source Code Copyright

All source code for this book is available under the Creative Commons Attribution 4.0 license, distributed via GitHub[3]. This is the official code distribution site. You may use this code in classroom and other educational situations as long as you cite this book as the source.

The primary goal of this copyright is to ensure that this book is properly cited and to prevent you from republishing the

---

[3]https://effectorientedprogramming.com/resources/zio/examples/2024-09-17

code without permission. As long as this book is cited, using examples from the book in most media is generally not a problem.

1.2.2: Invisible Code

We created a custom build system for this book. It ensures all examples are correct, or intentionally incorrect with the desired error messages. To keep the book examples focused, they are supported by invisible code that does not appear in the book. This invisible code is automatically extracted into the examples[4], so the cloned repository has everything you need. However, you can run the examples without understanding the invisible code.

1.3: Acknowledgements

Kit Langton, for being a kindred spirit in software interests and an inspiring contributor to the open source world.

Hali Frasure, for cooking so many dinners and elegantly facilitating our book nights.

Rumors Coffee and Townie Books in Crested Butte, CO, for being a place we like to hang out.

---

[4]https://effectorientedprogramming.com/resources/zio/examples/2024-09-17

2: Introduction

An *Effect* is an unpredictable interaction, usually with an external system. When a function uses an Effect, that function also becomes unpredictable.

For example, a function displaying the current date must ask for that information— usually from the operating system, which keeps track using a clock chip that lives outside the main processor. Such functions are unpredictable because you have no control over external system behavior.

2.1: Types of Effects

The impact of running an Effect is outside your control and cannot be undone:

- Printing a 3D figurine means you cannot reclaim that material.
- A blog post can be deleted after posting, but people might already have read it.
- Inserting a row into a database can cause multiple changes, even if you quickly delete that row.

There are many types of Effects:

- Accept user input
- Read from a file
- Get the current time from the system clock

- Generate a random number
- Display to a screen
- Write to a file
- Mutate a variable
- Interact with a database
- And more...

Effects have domain-specific forms:

- Get the current price of a stock
- Detect the electrical current from a pacemaker
- Check the temperature of a nuclear reactor
- Stabilize an airplane
- Trigger an alarm
- Sense slippage in an anti-lock braking system
- Detonate explosives

An *Effect System* manages Effects by wrapping these calls. You can change the behavior of Effects in a variety of ways that we show throughout the book. For example, you can feed data to an Effect to create reproducible tests.

The price you pay for these benefits is a fundamental change in the way you think about programming. Historically, this change has not been explained well. In this book, our goal is to ease this mental shift.

2.2: Motivation

For the past generation of languages, it made sense to focus on rapid development. You build a system as quickly as possible, then isolate failure points, finding and fixing bugs until the system is tolerable. You deliver tolerable systems rather than reliable systems.

Over the lifetime of a system, new needs are discovered and the system is adapted to meet those needs. Many of these adaptations don't conform to the original vision and architecture of the system. They must be forced into the system. Each forced feature degrades structure and integrity, making additional features even harder to force in. This degradation is commonly called *technical debt.* It's debt because you accumulate costs that are borne by future programmers. One day you hope to stop adding new features and pay down the accumulated debt by rewriting the system (this is called *refactoring*).

Often that debt never gets paid down. It becomes difficult or impossible to add new functionality. The system cannot be maintained and must be scrapped.

It is expensive and impractical to rewrite a system overwhelmed with debt. The costs are numerous, especially when the business cannot run without the software:

- For safety, you create the new system while also maintaining the old.
- You need an additional team to create the new system.
- You need programmers to maintain the existing system while the new system is developed.
- New functionality must be incorporated into both the old and new systems. You must continue forcing in new features as it gets harder and harder.
- The problems of software development are multiplied by (at least) two.

- In the end, the old system is discarded and the old-system team might become redundant. Being on that team is not a desirable job.
- You have no certainty if or when the new project succeeds.

We are now in an era where *modification of existing systems* is paramount. We always want rapid development, but we must adapt systems rather than rewrite them.

What if we could shift our thinking around the problem of building software systems? What if, when building a system from pieces, the parts were not buried within the whole? What if they are still accessible and changeable? The resulting system is far more adaptable.

2.3: The Pursuit of Adaptability

Imagine you want to create a system to build homes by assembling room modules. Each type of room has doors and windows, and there's a way to plug the room modules together. You select room modules with compatible doors and windows and assemble a house.

This concept of *composability* has been the prime objective of programming since we raised ourselves from the swamps of assembly language. We want to take smaller pieces and compose them into larger pieces, which are themselves composable. Over the decades, the programming community has made great strides in this endeavor. Each time we make a leap forward, however, we inevitably run into the next wall.

Our housing example is a reflection of where most programming is now: we have chunks of code—modules—and we put them together. We have improved our type systems and the ways we create data structures. What wall do we now face?

In the imaginary home-building system, we assemble rooms, but adding functionality to those rooms is expensive. If we want electricity in a room, we must tear up the walls and insert electrical conduits. To add a vent, we must tunnel through the building up to the roof. New plumbing must pass through the concrete foundation and the walls. For a room to do anything interesting, we must remodel the house.

Consider a software component that gets information from a server, processes it and then displays it. What happens if you incorporate this component and then discover the server is flaky? Perhaps it occasionally drops requests or takes too long. There are different strategies for this: retrying, backoff, querying other servers, etc. The problem is that, like the home-building system, you must go into the module and rebuild it. This takes time and effort and complicates the code. Instead, we want to easily attach new functionality without rewriting existing code.

In the home-building system, suppose each room contains a channel, and when you assemble room modules, the channels match up? If you want plumbing, electricity, venting, network cabling, etc., you run it through the channel. New features are added to rooms without rebuilding the house.

Effect Systems allow you to do the same thing for software as these channels could do for home-building: add features without rewriting the software.

2.4: What's Stopping Us?

We don't have the imaginary home-building system's "channel." To imagine what that channel would look like or how it behaves, we must examine some basic issues.

A dominant issue is *predictability*. Consider a simple function:

```scala
def p(a: Int, b: Int): Int =
  a + b
```

p is completely predictable:

- p(a, b) always produces an Int result.
- It never fails (assuming we don't run out of memory or hit rare system issues).
- The same inputs always produce the same outputs.
- It's so consistent that instead of calling the function, you can look up the results in a table—it is *cacheable*.

A predictable function has a special name: *pure*.

If we include something unpredictable in a pure function, the results become unpredictable. Here, we add a random number:

```scala
def u(a: Int, b: Int): Int =
  a + b + scala.util.Random.nextInt()
```

Not surprisingly, adding a random number to the result takes us from predictable to unpredictable. u never fails and always produces an Int, but if you call it twice with the same inputs, you get different outputs.

Unpredictable elements are *Side Effects*.

2.4.1: Side Effects

A Side Effect occurs when calling a function changes the context of that function. You don't just get a result from the function call, you mutate the surroundings. This might produce different behavior the next time you call the function. It can also change the behavior of the rest of the program.

We hope you wonder, "Isn't that what we've been talking about? Isn't that just an Effect?"

There's an important difference: Side Effects are unmanaged and Effects are managed. A Side Effect "just happens" but an Effect is explicitly tracked and controlled. For example, suppose you write to the console using the standard console library provided by your language. Writing to the console changes the surroundings because the output appears on the console. That's a Side Effect.

Mitigating the unpredictability of a traditional Side-Effecting function is messy and difficult. For this reason, the Effect System provides a special version of that function for performing Effects such as console I/O. That version tracks and manages the Side Effects. In the I/O example, the standard console library cannot control Side Effects, but the Effect library does.

2.5: Managing Effects

With an Effect System, we manage Effect behavior by putting that Effect in a kind of box. For example, instead of using `scala.util.Random`, we make our own random number generator:

```
def c(a: Int, b: Int): Int =
  a + b + ControlledRandom.nextInt()
```

`ControlledRandom` presumably uses `scala.util.Random`, but it could contain anything else. Now we can make the output of `ControlledRandom.nextInt()` predictable. For example, when testing `c` we can swap in a custom generator that produces controlled results.

An Effect System provides a set of components that replace Side-Effecting functions in standard libraries, along with the structure for managing Effectful functions that you write. An Effect System enables us to add almost any functionality to a program.

This requires a significant shift in the way you think about programming. It takes time and effort to rewire your brain into this new mode of thinking. This book gives you a gentle start along the path.

2.5.1: Deferred Execution

Managing an Effect means we not only control *what* results are produced by a function like `nextInt()`, but also *when* those results are produced. The control of *when* is called *deferred execution.* Deferred execution is part of the solution for easily attaching functionality to an existing program.

Consider the module that gets data from a server, processes it, then displays it. That sequence is executed as a single operation from the caller's perspective. Suppose the server we're trying to connect to is flaky. We'd like to add a retry, but we cannot directly access the server call because it is hidden behind a wall of code.

Let's treat the call to the server as an Effect. We manage it by putting a box around the server Effect like we did with `ControlledRandom`. The execution of that Effect is deferred, which means we can attach the retry (or another strategy such as a timeout) directly to that Effect.

Deferred execution adds a "cut point" where we modify the functionality of an Effect. Because Effects are the unpredictable points in a program, they comprise most of the places we want to modify functionality.

2.5.2: Minimal Effect Tracking

You have almost certainly seen `Unit`, `void`, or a similar construct in your preferred programming language. These are the bare minimum of Effect tracking.

Consider `saveInformation`, which has a type of `String => Unit`.

```
def saveInformation(info: String): Unit =
  ???
```

Returning `Unit` is the simplest indication of a Side-Effecting function. You don't call that function to produce a result value. Because of this, we know there must be a Side Effect—there's no other reason to call it.

A function without parameters is equivalent to a function with a `Unit` argument. No data flows into the function, so the only reason to call it is to produce a result. With no argument, the only thing that can produce a useful result is a Side Effect.

Thus, a function with either no arguments or a `Unit` return type is executed solely to perform Side Effects. This small hint is useful but not nearly as powerful as a true Effect System.

2.5.3: Failures

A function usually returns the expected answer, but there can be failures. Failures, especially reporting and handling them with exceptions, are another form of unpredictability.

Exceptions are not part of function return types. You cannot reliably know what exceptions might be thrown. Some languages tried using explicit *exception specifications*. These experiments did not improve composability.

An Effect System creates a structure as the return type from a function. This structure contains the expected answer along with every possible failure type. Failures become part of the type system. The type-checking system determines, from this return type, whether your code handles all possible failures.

The return type also includes the services the Effect depends on, which we explore later. This new return type provides the "channel" that enables easily adaptable systems.

2.6: Improving Your Life

Effect Systems make it easy to add functionality to existing systems. For example, you can add a timeout to any Effect to control its maximum duration. Applying such operations feels like a superpower, and that's what we show in the next chapter.

Learning Effect Systems requires patience. With most languages, you accumulate additional language features as standalone concepts. Effect Systems require a shift in perception of what code is and how it executes. We introduce Effect Systems in a way that is not overwhelming, to inspire you to keep working toward that shift.

3: Superpowers

Once programs are defined in terms of Effects, operations from the Effect System are applied to add new functionality. You do not need bespoke operations for different Effects. Common operations like `timeout` are applicable to all Effects while some operations like `retry` are only applicable to a subset of Effects. Operations can be chained.

Adapting your programs by applying operations to Effects feels like a superpower.

To illustrate, we show a few examples of common operations applied to Effects. We start by saving a user to a database and then gradually add superpowers. The act of saving is an Effect:

```
val userName = "Morty"

val effect0 =
  saveUser:
    userName
```

`effect0` is a `val` containing our Effect. Note that defining `effect0` does not execute that code—it only holds that code, to run at some later time. This is an example of *deferred execution*, described in the Introduction. Deferring the execution of an Effect is part of what enables us to add functionality to that Effect.

Effects are run as:

- "Main" programs
- Parts of larger programs
- Tests

To run an Effect as a "main" program, we extend the `ZIOAppDefault` trait provided by the ZIO library[1]:

```
import zio.*

object MyApp extends ZIOAppDefault:
  def run =
    Successful.simulate:
      effect0
```

The `def run` must be an Effect. `run` is special and passes the Effect to `ZIOAppDefault`, which runs it.

`Successful` is a `Scenario`, a device we created to simulate conditions needed by our examples. Scenarios let us execute Effects under these conditions. `Successful` is the "normal" scenario, so it doesn't introduce any special conditions. Throughout the book we create programs using scenarios to produce a variety of conditions, such as `DiskFull`, `TooCold` and even `NeverWorks`. You will see the results of using a scenario in the example output.

We also created helper code to reduce visual noise and shorten the application to:

```
def run =
  Successful.simulate:
    effect0
```

Output:

---

[1]`ZIO` also contains more specialized variations, but `ZIOAppDefault` is sufficient for this book.

```
Attempting to save user
Result: User saved
```

Because `effect0` runs in the Successful scenario, it does not fail.

In the WorksOnThirdTry scenario, the Effect does not work until the third try:

```
def run =
  WorksOnThirdTry.simulate:
    effect0
```

Output:

```
Attempting to save user
Log: **Database crashed!!**
Error: **Database crashed!!**
```

We only attempt `effect0` once, so this program fails, logging the failure information.

3.1: Retry

Sometimes things work if you keep trying. We retry `effect0` by attaching the `retryN` operation:

```
val effect1 = effect0.retryN(2)
```

With few exceptions, applying an operation to an Effect produces a new Effect. This new Effect also has delayed execution.

Here, we assign the new Effect `effect0.retryN` to a `val`, creating `effect1`. In `effect1`, `effect0` is tried once, then retried two more times, so it works on the third try:

```
def run =
  WorksOnThirdTry.simulate:
    effect1
```

Output:

```
Attempting to save user
Log: **Database crashed!!**
Attempting to save user
Log: **Database crashed!!**
Attempting to save user
Result: User saved
```

3.1.1: The `NeverWorks` Scenario

With `NeverWorks`, the Effect fails its initial attempt and any
further retries:

```
def run =
  NeverWorks.simulate:
    effect1
```

Output:

```
Attempting to save user
Log: **Database crashed!!**
Attempting to save user
Log: **Database crashed!!**
Attempting to save user
Log: **Database crashed!!**
Error: **Database crashed!!**
```

3.2: Modifying Failure

So the user doesn't see the crashing database, `orElseFail`
transforms the failure into a user-friendly message:

```
val effect2 =
  effect1.orElseFail:
    "FAILURE: User not saved"
```

orElseFail is attached to the prior effect1 containing the retry. effect2 is a new Effect that performs the retry and converts any failures into the error message. Running this new Effect in the NeverWorks scenario fails with our new message:

```
def run =
  NeverWorks.simulate:
    effect2
```

Output:

```
Attempting to save user
Log: **Database crashed!!**
Attempting to save user
Log: **Database crashed!!**
Attempting to save user
Log: **Database crashed!!**
Error: FAILURE: User not saved
```

The behavior is altered without restructuring the original Effect.

3.3: Timeout

With retries, you saw the Effect fail quickly. Sometimes an Effect fails by taking too long.

timeoutFail can be chained to our previous Effect to control the maximum time the Effect runs. timeoutFail takes two arguments; we pass the first using parentheses, and the second uses significant indentation. We prefer significant indentation, but sometimes parentheses increase readability.

```
val effect3 =
  effect2
    .timeoutFail("** Save timed out **"):
      5.seconds
```

Timeouts can be added to any Effect.

The Slow scenario runs longer than our specified time limit of five seconds:

```
def run =
  Slow.simulate:
    effect3
```

Output:

```
Attempting to save user
Error: ** Save timed out **
```

Because the Effect does not complete within the time limit, it is canceled and fails. The retry behavior in effect1 does not occur because it only activates when the inner operation fails. If you want to retry when the timeout occurs, attach the retryN operation after timeoutFail.

3.4: Fallback

A failing Effect can fall back to a different strategy using orElse:

```
val effect4 =
  effect3.orElse:
    sendToManualQueue:
      userName
```

sendToManualQueue happens when the user cannot be saved (i.e., when effect3 fails). This displays a message indicating the new user must be manually provisioned.

We run the new Effect in the NeverWorks scenario to ensure we reach the fallback:

```
def run =
  NeverWorks.simulate:
    effect4
```

Output:

```
Attempting to save user
Log: **Database crashed!!**
Attempting to save user
Log: **Database crashed!!**
Attempting to save user
Log: **Database crashed!!**
Result: Sent Morty to manual queue
```

The retries do not succeed, so the fallback is applied.

3.5: Finalization

To ensure that a desired behavior happens after an Effect completes, even if it fails, we can attach withFinalizer to any Effect:

```
val effect5 =
  effect4.withFinalizer:
    username => logUserSignup(username)
```

`withFinalizer` expects a function as its argument. In this case, our finalizer logs that a user signed up. `withFinalizer` attaches this behavior without changing the error or result types of the original Effect.

```
def run =
  Successful.simulate:
    effect5
```

Output:

```
Attempting to save user
Log: Signup initiated for Morty
Result: User saved
```

Behavior can be added to an Effect regardless of that Effect's failure and success types.

3.6: Timing

For diagnostic information, you can track timing:

```
val effect6 = effect5.timed
```

```
def run =
  Successful.simulate:
    effect6
```

Output:

```
Attempting to save user
Log: Signup initiated for Morty
Result: (PT0.002206111S,User saved)
```

When running the Effect in the `Successful` scenario, the timing information is packaged with the original output `String`.

3.7: Filtering

Our lead engineer tells us Morty should be prevented from using our system. The `when` excludes Morty:

```
val effect7 =
  effect6.when(userName != "Morty")
```

```
def run =
  Successful.simulate:
    effect7
```

Output:

```
Result: None
```

We added this behavior to the *end* of a complex Effect. Consider the work necessary to do this without an Effect System.

3.8: Effects are the Sum of Their Parts

These examples are a glimpse of the superpowers you can add to *any* Effect. We started with:

- `effect0`: Save User

Effects 1–7 are new Effects, each built on the previous Effect:

- `effect1`: Retry
- `effect2`: Modifying Failure
- `effect3`: Timeout
- `effect4`: Fallback
- `effect5`: Logging
- `effect6`: Timing
- `effect7`: Filtering

Each Effect is independent, and there are many other behaviors we can attach. You can mix and match retries, fallbacks, etc. You can create new Effects with additional superpowers.

3.9: Deferred Execution

If Effects ran immediately, we could not freely add behaviors:

- We cannot timeout something that is already running, or already completed.
- We cannot retry something if we only hold the completed result.
- We cannot parallelize operations if they have already started single-threaded execution.

When we manage an Effect, we hold a value that represents something that *can* be run but hasn't yet. Deferred execution allows the Effect System to freely add behavior before or after that value.

Because Effects are deferred and independent, we can combine them in a variety of ways. A fundamental way to combine Effects is sequentially. You might think this should work:

```
def run =
  Successful.simulate:
    ZIO.debug("Before save")
    effect1
```

Output:

```
Attempting to save user
Result: User saved
```

The result returned by `run` is `effect1`, which is the final value of the function. The Effect System takes `effect1` returned by `run` and only runs that. Since Effects are deferred, `ZIO.debug` never runs. It is an unused `val`, the same as dropping a `String` or `Int` that you never use into the middle of a block.

To sequence multiple Effects, we construct a new `Effect`. We assign this new Effect to a `val` like we did with `effect1`-`effect7`:

```
val effect8 =
  defer:
    ZIO.debug("Before save").run
    effect1.run
```

Within a defer we create a sequence of Effects by applying
.run to each Effect. A defer block creates a new Effect
containing the sequence. The .run method is only available
to Effects within a defer block.

The new Effect now produces the output from ZIO.debug:

```
def run =
  Successful.simulate:
    effect8
```

Output:

```
Before save
Attempting to save user
Result: User saved
```

3.9.1: The .run Method

The two versions of run seem confusing, but they serve
different purposes:

- Assigning an Effect to def run executes that Effect as
  the program. This typically happens only once in an
  application.
- Attaching .run to Effects in a defer establishes the
  order of execution for that Effect. This can happen many
  times throughout a program.

Calling .run on anything other than an Effect produces a
compiler error:

```
val program =
  defer:
    "hello".run
```

Output:

```
error:
value run is not a member of String.
```

Once you .run an Effect, we cannot call further ZIO methods on it:

```
val programManipulatingBeforeRun =
  defer:
    effect8.run.repeatN(3)
```

Output:

```
error:
value repeatN is not a member of String.
```

Running an Effect using .run produces its result, not the deferred computation. Thus, there's no appropriate place to attach repeatN(3).

We can nest behavior to any depth, placing deferred Effects within other deferred Effects:

```
def run =
  Successful.simulate:
    defer:
      ZIO.debug("**Before**").run
      effect8.debug.repeatN(1).run
      ZIO.debug("**After**").run
```

Output:

```
**Before**
Before save
Attempting to save user
User saved
Before save
Attempting to save user
User saved
**After**
```

Deferred execution might seem strange at first, but it is
essential for inserting new functionality into Effects.

4: Initialization

Initializing an application from values provided at startup is a perennial challenge. Solutions are diverse, impressive and often bewildering.

Dependency Inversion means building an application from modules and using abstractions to express what those modules need. These abstractions allow us to use *dependency injection* to provide those dependencies using startup values. Traditionally, we manually construct and hard-wire the dependencies, making configuration costly and difficult. Dependency injection automatically creates and provides instances of those dependencies. This produces more flexible systems.

Common approaches to dependency injection rely on runtime inspection, typically using reflection. This requires that all dependencies be created through a dependency injection manager. Runtime dependency injection is complicated and can make it difficult or impossible to express dependencies at compile time.

With Effects, the type system expresses dependencies and the compiler ensures the necessary parts are available.

4.1: Effects and Dependencies

Managing dependencies using Effects yields valuable compile-time benefits. Services are defined as classes with constructor arguments, just as in an ordinary Scala application. When building the application, these services are provided in a single flat space. Each component automatically locates its dependencies while also making itself available to other components.

There are two primary reasons an Effect System includes dependencies:

1. Dependencies are easily changed between local development, production and tests.
2. Dependency state is managed outside the Effect.

Dependency cycles are not allowed by ZIO—you cannot build a program where A depends on B, and B depends on A. You are alerted at compile time about illegal cycles.

ZIO's dependency management provides capabilities that are not possible in other approaches. For example, you can share a single instance of a dependency across multiple test classes, or even multiple applications. See more details in the ZIO docs[1].

4.2: Defining Dependencies

The following series of examples shows how we can change dependencies to meet different needs for making Bread. Because the Bread is provided in multiple ways (the store, bake it from scratch, etc.), we define it as a trait:

---

[1]https://effectorientedprogramming.com/resources/zio/sharing-layers

```
trait Bread:
  val eat = ZIO.debug("Bread: Eating")
```

Bread's single eat Effect simulates an action on the Bread by displaying a debug message. Next, we need an implementation of Bread:

```
class BreadStoreBought extends Bread
```

Because BreadStoreBought is a type of Bread, we can provide it to any Effect that needs Bread. To provide Bread-StoreBought as a dependency, we wrap it in a special kind of Effect called a ZLayer:

```
ZLayer.succeed:
  BreadStoreBought()
```

The Effect System uses ZLayers to automatically build and inject dependencies. An essential difference between ZLayers and other dependency injection systems is that a ZLayer validates dependencies *at compile time.* If you do something problematic, the build system and/or IDE immediately provide a useful error message.

4.3: Effects as Dependencies

We define a new Effect that displays a message and creates a BreadStoreBought instance:

```
val purchaseBread =
  defer:
    ZIO.debug("Buying bread").run
    BreadStoreBought()
```

`ZLayer.fromZIO` creates a `ZLayer` from an Effect, in this case our `purchaseBread` Effect:

```
val storeBoughtBread =
  ZLayer.fromZIO:
    purchaseBread
```

`storeBoughtBread` creates a `BreadStoreBought` instance and turns it into a successful `ZLayer` Effect to provide a `Bread` dependency.

It can also be convenient to put the function producing a `ZLayer` in a companion object.

You can think of a `ZLayer` as a more-powerful constructor. Like `ZIO` Effects, `ZLayer`s are deferred, so merely referencing `storeBoughtBread` does not construct anything.

At this point we have:

- The `Bread` trait.
- A `Bread` implementation—`BreadStoreBought`.
- An Effect that creates the instance of `BreadStore-Bought`.
- The `ZLayer` that produces `BreadStoreBought` as a dependency for any Effect that needs it.

4.4: Providing Dependencies to Effects

Here's an Effect that has a `Bread` dependency:

```
val eatBread =
  ZIO.serviceWithZIO[Bread]:
    bread => bread.eat
```

`serviceWithZIO` takes a type parameter, which is the service it needs to do the work. Here, `serviceWithZIO[Bread]` says, "I need an instance that implements `trait Bread` and I will create a new Effect with it." The argument to `serviceWithZIO[Bread]` is the function that does the work using the provided dependency. A *lambda* is a nameless function that uses => to separate parameters from the function body. The instance it receives from `serviceWithZIO` becomes the `bread` parameter in the lambda.

We make the function call by passing a *service* as an argument instead of passing that argument directly. Because that argument is an abstraction, it can be provided during initialization.

Services are supplied during initialization using the `provide` method. This uses one or more `ZLayer`s to produce the necessary item—in this case some type of `Bread`—which is passed to the lambda `bread => bread.eat`.

`eatBread` has a dependency on `Bread`, so to run the Effect we must `provide` a `ZLayer` that constructs a `Bread`:

```
def run =
  eatBread.provide:
    storeBoughtBread
```

Output:

```
Buying bread
Bread: Eating
```

Code like this can be written without using ZLayers, but as dependencies become more complex, systems rapidly become unmanageable. ZLayers keep everything organized and ensure that all dependencies are provided and correct.

To run an Effect, first `provide` all required dependencies. Leaving out a dependency produces a compiler error:

```
eatBread.provide()
```

Output:

```
──── ZLAYER ERROR ────────────

 Please provide a layer for:

   1. Bread

```

The error shows exactly what you're missing—and you see this error in your IDE as you write the code. Traditional dependency injection systems cannot discover until runtime if you're missing something. Even then, they typically cannot know for sure if you've successfully provided all dependencies.

4.5: Dependencies With Dependencies

Instead of buying bread, let's make it. First we create Dough:

```
class Dough:
  val letRise = ZIO.debug("Dough: rising")
```

Dependencies can be Effects, primitives, custom types, unions, etc.

The recommended pattern defines ZLayers in the companion object:

```
object Dough:
  val fresh =
    ZLayer.fromZIO:
      defer:
        ZIO.debug("Dough: Mixed").run
        Dough()
```

Looking at the code from the inside out, the defer block executes ZIO.debug by calling .run on the Effect. Dough() is a pure expression, so it is returned directly without calling .run on it. A defer block always creates an Effect; in this case that Effect produces Dough. The defer Effect is passed to ZLayer.fromZIO which produces a ZLayer providing a Dough instance.

Once the Dough has risen, we want to bake it. For this we define a HeatSource:

```
trait HeatSource
```

Our first HeatSource is an Oven:

```
class Oven extends HeatSource

object Oven:
  val heated =
    ZLayer.fromZIO:
      defer:
        ZIO.debug("Oven: Heated").run
        Oven()
```

`Oven.heated` is a `ZLayer` that provides an `Oven` as a `HeatSource`. We can use this `HeatSource` to bake `Bread`.

Now we define the dependencies for `BreadHomeMade`:

```
class BreadHomeMade(
    heat: HeatSource,
    dough: Dough,
) extends Bread

val homeMadeBread =
  ZLayer.fromZIO:
    defer:
      ZIO.debug("BreadHomeMade: Baked").run
      BreadHomeMade(
        ZIO.service[Oven].run,
        ZIO.service[Dough].run,
      )
```

`homeMadeBread` is a `ZLayer` that provides `BreadHomeMade`, which has two dependencies, `Oven` and `Dough`. The `ZIO.service` calls say, "I need an `Oven`" and "I need `Dough`." The Effect System ensures those services are found.

We pass the previous `eatBread` Effect to `run`, this time using the `homeMadeBread` layer along with its dependencies:

```
def run =
  eatBread.provide(
    homeMadeBread,
    Dough.fresh,
    Oven.heated,
  )
```

Output:

```
Oven: Heated
Dough: Mixed
BreadHomeMade: Baked
Bread: Eating
```

eatBread requires Bread, which is satisfied by homeMade-
Bread. But homeMadeBread, in turn, needs the services
Dough.fresh and Oven.heated. If we do not include all necessary services in the provide arguments, the type checker
produces helpful error messages; try removing a service to
see this.

4.6: Naming Dependencies

Effects are actions, so they have verb names, e.g., eat and
purchaseBread. The ZLayer is the structure that provides
an instance to your application. This instance is a thing.
Thus, the name of a ZLayer should be a noun, e.g., Bread-
StoreBought. Inside the companion object we typically use
an adjective for the method that produces the ZLayer, e.g.,
storeBought and homeMade. However, the name of the
companion object (Bread) *together* with the adjective still
produces a noun:

```
object Bread:
  val storeBought = storeBoughtBread
  val homeMade    = homeMadeBread
```

We use this in the remaining examples.

4.7: Sharing Dependencies

Next, we'd like to make Toast from Bread. Toast is a trait
because we need different kinds:

```
trait Toast:
  val bread: Bread
  val heat: HeatSource
  val eat = ZIO.debug("Toast: Eating")
```

A Toast implementation requires a HeatSource and Bread:

```
case class ToastFromHeatSource(
    bread: Bread,
    heat: HeatSource,
) extends Toast

object ToastFromHeatSource:
  val toasted =
    ZLayer.fromZIO:
      defer:
        ZIO.debug("Toast: Made").run
        ToastFromHeatSource(
          ZIO.service[Bread].run,
          ZIO.service[HeatSource].run,
        )
```

A Toaster can be the HeatSource to make Toast:

```scala
class Toaster extends HeatSource

object Toaster:
  val ready =
    ZLayer.fromZIO:
      defer:
        ZIO.debug("Toaster: Ready").run
        Toaster()
```

Now we have all necessary services to make and eat Toast:

```scala
def run =
  ZIO
    .serviceWithZIO[Toast]:
      toast => toast.eat
    .provide(
      ToastFromHeatSource.toasted,
      Dough.fresh,
      Bread.homeMade,
      Oven.heated,
      Toaster.ready,
    )
```

Output:

```
────── ZLAYER ERROR ───────────

 Ambiguous layers!

   HeatSource is provided by:
     1. Oven.heated
     2. Toaster.ready,

───────────────────────────
```

Both Oven and Toaster are HeatSources, so trying to include Toaster.ready produces an ambiguity error. If we remove Toaster.ready, the program uses the Oven for both HeatSources. This works, but it is inefficient to heat an oven to make toast.

To solve this problem, introduce more specific types. Here, ToastFromToaster specifies a Toaster rather than an arbitrary HeatSource:

```
case class ToastFromToaster(
    bread: Bread,
    heat: Toaster,
) extends Toast

object ToastFromToaster:
  val toasted =
    ZLayer.fromZIO:
      defer:
        ZIO.debug("Toast: Made").run
        ToastFromToaster(
          ZIO.service[Bread].run,
          ZIO.service[Toaster].run,
        )
```

Now the Oven bakes the Bread and the Toaster makes the Toast. This Effect makes Toast and eats it:

```
def run =
  ZIO
    .serviceWithZIO[Toast]:
      toast => toast.eat
    .provide(
      ToastFromToaster.toasted,
      Dough.fresh,
      Bread.homeMade,
      // The two HeatSources don't clash:
      Oven.heated,
      Toaster.ready,
    )
```

Output:

```
Toaster: Ready
Oven: Heated
Dough: Mixed
BreadHomeMade: Baked
Toast: Made
Toast: Eating
```

The order of the `provide` arguments is unimportant.

Try rewriting the example using `BreadStoreBought`.

4.8: The Dependency Graph

The interrelationships in `provide` are called the *dependency graph.* To generate a dependency graph, add `ZLayer.Debug.tree` to `provide`:

```
def run =
  ZIO
    .serviceWithZIO[Toast]:
      toast => toast.eat
    .provide(
      ZLayer.Debug.tree,
      ToastFromToaster.toasted,
      Dough.fresh,
      Bread.homeMade,
      Oven.heated,
      Toaster.ready,
    )
```

Output:

```
Toaster: Ready
Oven: Heated
Dough: Mixed
BreadHomeMade: Baked
Toast: Made
Toast: Eating
```

```
ZLayer Dependency Graph
◻ ToastFromToaster.toasted
├◻ Toaster.ready
◻─◻ Bread.homeMade
   ├◻ Oven.heated
   ◻─◻ Dough.fresh
```

ToastFromToaster requires a Toaster and Bread. To provide Bread.homeMade, we need Dough and an Oven.

In most dependency injection systems, the dependency graph is resolved for you. This typically happens in a special startup phase that attempts to discover dependencies by following code paths. Such systems don't always detect all dependencies, and the ones they find aren't visible until runtime. ZIO's compile-time focus means you discover problems as you write code, saving time and preventing production issues.

4.9: Dependency Cleanup

Our basic Oven contains a dangerous oversight: we heat it up, but never turn it off! We solve the problem using withFinalizer, briefly introduced in the Superpowers chapter. When no longer needed, an OvenSafe turns itself off:

```
object OvenSafe:
  val heated =
    ZLayer.scoped:
      defer:
        ZIO.debug("Oven: Heated").run
        Oven()
      .withFinalizer:
        _ => ZIO.debug("Oven: Turning off")
```

Here, scoped produces a ZLayer with a finalizer attached to the Oven instance it provides. When that Oven becomes unused, the finalizer automatically runs.

We substitute OvenSafe into our bread-making provisions:

```
def run =
  eatBread.provide(
    Bread.homeMade,
    Dough.fresh,
    OvenSafe.heated,
  )
```

Output:

```
Oven: Heated
Dough: Mixed
BreadHomeMade: Baked
Bread: Eating
Oven: Turning off
```

When you procure an OvenSafe via its heated ZLayer, that Oven turns itself off after its last use.

4.10: Construction Failure

Dependencies can contain Effects, so dependencies can fail.

We have a `Friend` (implementation hidden) who sometimes gives us Bread. They don't always answer the first time we try to contact them:

```
def run =
  eatBread.provide:
    ZLayer.fromZIO:
      Friend.requestBread
```

Output:

```
Attempt 1: Failure(Friend Unreachable)
Error: Failure(Friend Unreachable)
```

The program fails because it cannot get `Bread` from our `Friend` on the first try.

4.10.1: Fallback Dependencies

If our `Friend` has no `Bread` to give us, we can set up a fallback strategy using `orElse`:

```
def run =
  eatBread.provide:
    ZLayer
      .fromZIO:
        Friend.requestBread
      .orElse:
        Bread.storeBought
```

Output:

```
Attempt 1: Failure(Friend Unreachable)
Buying bread
Bread: Eating
```

If we cannot get `Bread` from our `Friend`, we go to the store and buy it.

4.10.2: Retries

`Friend.requestBread` is an Effect. This means we can apply Effect operations. For example, we can add a retry to the `Effect` produced by `Friend.requestBread`:

```
def run =
  eatBread.provide:
    ZLayer.fromZIO:
      Friend.requestBread.retryN(1)
```

Output:

```
Attempt 1: Failure(Friend Unreachable)
Attempt 2: Failure(Friend Unreachable)
Error: Failure(Friend Unreachable)
```

We didn't try our unreliable friend enough times to get `Bread` but we did make an initial attempt and a subsequent retry.

In a real application, you might provide the number of retries as a `ZLayer` so you can change it in different environments. We use a case class to hold configuration information:

```
case class RetryConfig(times: Int)
```

The `configurableBread` ZLayer requires a `RetryConfig` and provides `Bread`:

```
val configurableBread =
  ZLayer.fromZIO:
    defer:
      val config =
        ZIO.service[RetryConfig].run
      Friend
        .requestBread
        .retryN:
          config.times
        .run
```

We first provide a static `RetryConfig` to eatBread:

```
val retryTwice =
  ZLayer.succeed:
    RetryConfig(2)

def run =
  eatBread
    .provide(configurableBread, retryTwice)
```

Output:

```
Attempt 1: Failure(Friend Unreachable)
Attempt 2: Failure(Friend Unreachable)
Attempt 3: Failure(Friend Unreachable)
Error: Failure(Friend Unreachable)
```

This is still not enough attempts to get `Bread` from our
`Friend`. We could keep increasing this value and rebuilding
the program, but this is not practical in real applications. We
want to modify the number of retries based on an external
configuration.

4.11: External Configuration

Programs often configure their behavior based on values provided at startup. There are three common approaches:

- Command-line arguments
- Configuration files
- OS environment variables

We need a type that converts a configuration into a `RetryConfig`. We can automatically create a *descriptor* using the `deriveConfig` macro from the `zio.config.magnolia` module:

```
import zio.config.magnolia.deriveConfig

val configDescriptor =
  deriveConfig[RetryConfig]
```

We need a configuration format to provide to the descriptor. HOCON stands for *Human-Optimized Configuration Object Notation*. This is a text-based, key-value format similar to JSON. Normally, we would read the configuration from a file, but we want to keep the example self-contained. Here, `configProvider` is initialized from a HOCON string in the code:

```
import zio.config.*
import zio.config.typesafe.*

val configProvider =
  ConfigProvider.fromHoconString:
    "{ times: 3 }"
```

We use `configDescriptor` and `configProvider` together
to fully describe how to acquire and transform the data. `read`
then captures that behavior in an Effect executed during layer
construction:

```
val configuration =
  ZLayer.fromZIO:
    read:
      configDescriptor.from:
        configProvider
```

Now `configuration` is a ZLayer we provide to `eatBread`:

```
def run =
  eatBread.provide(
    configurableBread,
    configuration,
  )
```

Output:

```
Attempt 1: Failure(Friend Unreachable)
Attempt 2: Failure(Friend Unreachable)
Attempt 3: Failure(Friend Unreachable)
Attempt 4: Succeeded
Bread: Eating
```

After an initial attempt and three retries we get our bread from a `Friend` and eat it.

`zio.config` gives easy access to configuration data, solving a common requirement in real-world applications. Find further details in the ZIO Config documentation[2].

---

[2]http://effectorientedprogramming.com/resources/zio/zio-config-docs-index

5: Testing

Testing requires predictability, but Effects that access external systems are unpredictable. To create predictable tests, Effect Systems let you swap the external systems with your own, controlled, sources. You can insert these controlled sources because Effects are isolated, accessible, and use delayed execution.

Anything an Effect needs (from the system or the environment) can be substituted in tests for something predictable. For example, an Effect that fetches users from a database can use simulated data without creating a test database.

To easily replace external systems during testing, we supply a test implementation via a `ZLayer` (covered in the Initialization chapter). The `provide` method allows us to provide `ZLayer`s for different scenarios: testing, debugging, running normally, etc.

5.1: Basic ZIO Testing

A test must return an `Assertion`. To create a test, import elements from `zio.test` and create an `object` that extends `ZIOSpecDefault` with a `spec` function:

```
object Basic extends ZIOSpecDefault:
  def spec =
    test("Basic"):
      assertTrue(1 == 1)
```

The `String` argument to `test` is displayed in the test report.

Note that the final expression is the `Assertion` `assertTrue`. Because of its power and flexibility, you'll normally use assertTrue. However, there are numerous other `Assertions` in the test library[1].

For this book, we created a test helper similar to our application helper:

```
def spec =
  test("Basic"):
    assertTrue(1 == 1)
```

Output:

```
+ Basic
```

Successful test cases start with a + and failed test cases start with a -.

`Assertions` are pure expressions, not statements. This means `Assertions` that *are not* at the end of the test will not do anything. Only the final `Assertion` in a test is returned to the test framework:

---

[1]https://effectorientedprogramming.com/resources/zio/test-assertion-library

```
def spec =
  test("Only the last assertTrue matters"):
    assertTrue(1 != 1) // Ignored
    assertTrue(1 == 1)
```

Output:

```
+ Only the last assertTrue matters
```

If you are accustomed to side-effecting assertions, this requires a mental adjustment. It is possible to write a test that "passes" but does not execute the assertions you think it does. Most development tools warn you about the unused assertion value.

To put multiple Boolean evaluations within a single `assertTrue`, separate them with commas:

```
def spec =
  test("Multiple Boolean expressions"):
    assertTrue(1 == 1, 2 == 2, 3 == 3)
```

Output:

```
+ Multiple Boolean expressions
```

To combine multiple `assertTrue` expressions, use `&&` and `||`:

```
def spec =
  test("Combine using operators"):
    assertTrue(1 == 0) ||
    assertTrue(2 == 2) &&
    assertTrue(3 == 3)
```

Output:

```
+ Combine using operators
```

To negate an assertTrue expression, use !:

```
def spec =
  test("negation"):
    !assertTrue(42 == 47)
```

Output:

```
+ negation
```

An Effect is a test as long as the final expression of that Effect is an Assertion. The Effect is automatically run by the test framework:

```
def spec =
  test("Effect as test"):
    defer:
      ZIO.debug("Executing logic").run
      assertCompletes
```

Output:

```
Executing logic
+ Effect as test
```

The `defer` produces an Effect that runs `ZIO.debug`, then returns `assertCompletes` which unconditionally indicates that everything ran successfully.

Here is a reusable test that takes a parameter, runs an Effect, and validates that it completes:

```
def showLabel(label: String) =
  defer:
    ZIO.debug(s"Running $label").run
    assertCompletes
```

We assign the Effect to a `val` and use that as the test logic:

```
val effectA = showLabel("A")
```

```
def spec =
  test("Case A"):
    effectA
```

Output:

```
Running A
+ Case A
```

Tests are typically collected into a `suite`. The tests in a `suite` run as a group:

```
val effectB = showLabel("B")

def spec =
  suite("Suite of Tests")(
    test("Case A in suite")(effectA),
    test("Case B in suite")(effectB),
  )
```

Output:

```
Running A
Running B
+ Suite of Tests
  + Case A in suite
  + Case B in suite
```

Tests run in parallel by default, so the output does not necessarily appear in the order the tests are listed.

We can store complete test cases in `val`s:

```
import zio.test.test

def testCase(label: String) =
  test(s"Case $label in a value"):
    showLabel(label)



val testA = testCase("A")
val testB = testCase("B")



def spec =
  suite("A Suite of Tests")(testA, testB)
```

Output:

```
Running A
Running B
+ A Suite of Tests
  + Case A in a value
  + Case B in a value
```

Notice the flexibility this allows. Traditionally, you must compromise between concise tests and the clarity of the test output. Do you want to write one test with 100 assertions or 100 tests with one assertion each? The first is concise and quick to write, but failures are hard to read. The second clearly shows what failed but requires significant boilerplate. An Effect Oriented test library produces the best of both worlds by generating tests programmatically.

5.2: Test Dependencies

Suppose you want to build birdhouses, and you have a choice of materials and `Nailers` for building them. The `Materials` have different levels of `brittleness`, so some `Nailers` might break some `Materials`. We want to test different `Materials` with different `Nailers`. All `Materials` and `Nailers` have `ZLayer` services that are easily swapped during testing.

`Wood` and `Plastic` are `Materials` with different `brittleness` factors:

```
case class Material(brittleness: Int)

object Material:
  val wood =
    ZLayer.succeed:
      Material(brittleness = 5)
  val plastic =
    ZLayer.succeed:
      Material(brittleness = 10)
```

Nailers have a force that relates to Material.brittleness:

```
case class Nailer(force: Int)

object Nailer:
  val hand =
    ZLayer.succeed:
      Nailer(force = 4)

  val robotic =
    ZLayer.succeed:
      Nailer(force = 11)
```

testNailerWithMaterial takes a Material and checks it against a Nailer:

```
val testNailerWithMaterial =
  defer:
    val material = ZIO.service[Material].run
    val nailer   = ZIO.service[Nailer].run
    assertTrue(
      nailer.force < material.brittleness
    )
```

Notice that all dependencies are unfulfilled. This way, each test can provide different combinations of services:

```
def spec =
  suite("Construction Combinations")(
    test("Wood with hand nailer"):
      testNailerWithMaterial
        .provide(Material.wood, Nailer.hand)
    ,
    test("Plastic with hand nailer"):
      testNailerWithMaterial.provide(
        Material.plastic,
        Nailer.hand,
      )
    ,
    test("Plastic with robo nailer"):
      testNailerWithMaterial.provide(
        Material.plastic,
        Nailer.robotic,
      ),
  )
```

Output:

```
+ Construction Combinations
  + Wood with hand nailer
  + Plastic with hand nailer
  - Plastic with robo nailer
    ☐ 11 was not less than 10
    nailer.force < material.brittleness
    .force = 11
    nailer = Nailer(force = 11)
```

Notice the clarity of the failure report—it shows exactly what's happening.

As an exercise, try adding a new `Material` called `Metal`.

5.3: Testing Built-Ins

As you've just seen, whenever you create a type, you can include a method to produce a ZLayer containing an instance of that type. To vary the types across multiple tests, supply different types to each test using provide.

This only works for user-defined types. What about built-in types like Random and Clock? For these, ZIO Test provides special APIs.

5.3.1: Randomness

Randomness is intentionally unpredictable. When testing, we treat randomness as an Effect and swap in our own sequence of numbers. The following coinToss function uses Random.nextBoolean from the ZIO library. The .run at the end tells you that this must be an Effect, and not a call to scala.util.Random:

```
val coinToss =
  defer:
    if Random.nextBoolean.run then
      ZIO.debug("Heads").run
      ZIO.succeed("Heads").run
    else
      ZIO.debug("Tails").run
      ZIO.fail("Tails").run
```

The if looks at whether nextBoolean is true or false and produces a successful Heads or a failing Tails accordingly.

Now we use coinToss to fill a List with five tosses:

```
val flipFive =
  defer:
    ZIO
      .collectAllSuccesses:
        List.fill(5):
          coinToss
      .run
      .size
```

collectAllSuccesses tells us how many tosses are ZIO.succeed("Heads"). Note that collectAllSuccesses is not looking at true versus false values, but rather succeed versus fail objects. After .run, the .size produces the number of succeed Effects as an Int.

Running this using the built-in, side-effecting Random.nextBoolean, we see the expected random assortment of Heads and Tails:

```
def run =
  flipFive
```

Output:

```
Heads
Tails
Tails
Heads
Tails
Result: 2
```

Random.nextBoolean fetches the next random Boolean value from the source of randomness. With scala.util.Random this source is hardwired into the function, but with ZIO we can feed numbers to Random.nextBoolean using TestRandom.feedBooleans:

```
def spec =
  test("Flip 5 times"):
    defer:
      TestRandom
        .feedBooleans(true, true, true)
        .run
      TestRandom
        .feedBooleans(false, false)
        .run
      val heads =
        flipFive.debug("Number of Heads").run
      assertTrue(heads == 3)
```

Output:

```
Tails
Tails
Heads
Heads
Heads
Number of Heads: 3
+ Flip 5 times
```

We first feed three `true` booleans followed by two `false` booleans, but these are ordered last-in-first-out so we see the `Tails` first in the output.

Our use of `TestRandom.feedBooleans` might seem disconnected from the `coinToss` used for `flipFive`. But `coinToss` asks for random numbers, and `TestRandom.feedBooleans` provides them. Even though `coinToss` is buried in other functions, its behavior can still be controlled to produce a consistent test.

In the absence of "random" booleans fed from `TestRandom.feedBooleans`, `coinToss` uses a pseudorandom value.

If something in a system needs random numbers, you can use the default behavior, or you can provide your own sequence using `TestRandom`. When randomness is an Effect, testing unpredictable scenarios is straightforward—you transparently provide data that produces deterministic behavior.

5.3.2: Time

Because the clock is an Effect, time can be simulated during testing. Suppose we want to parse accumulated CSV files every 24 hours:

```
val nightlyBatch =
  ZIO.sleep(24.hours).debug("Parsing CSV")
```

When using ZIO Test, the clock does not move forward on its own; you must explicitly change it. Unless you move the time forward, calling a time-based Effect like `timeout` hangs indefinitely with the message:

```
Warning: A test is using time, but is not
advancing the test clock, which may result
in the test hanging. Use TestClock.adjust
to manually advance the time.
```

Note that the Effect System can detect that the clock is not moving forward and issue a warning. This impressive feat is not possible with many other programming systems.

To advance the `TestClock`, call `adjust`:

```
val timeTravel =
  TestClock.adjust:
    24.hours
```

It won't work to call `adjust` before or after we execute
`nightlyBatch`. We must move the clock *while nightly-
Batch is running*—that is, in parallel. We achieve this with
`zipPar`, though other methods are available if more low-level
control is needed:

```
def spec =
  test("Batch runs after 24 hours"):
    defer:
      nightlyBatch.zipPar(timeTravel).run
      assertCompletes
```

Output:

```
Parsing CSV: ()
+ Batch runs after 24 hours
```

Here, `zipPar` runs `nightlyBatch` and `timeTravel` in parallel. This ensures that `nightlyBatch` completes by moving
the clock forward 24 hours. The test runs in milliseconds
instead of a real-world day.

Using a simulated clock means we no longer rely on real-
world time. Tests are also more predictable because time
adjustments are fully controlled.

5.3.2.1: Targeting Failure-Prone Time Bands

Using real-world time is error-prone because Effects have
unexpected results in certain time bands. Consider fetching

a time that happens to be 23:59:59. After performing some operations, you get database records for the current day. Those records may no longer be from the day associated with previously received records. This scenario can be tough to test when using real-world time. With a simulated clock, your tests adjust the clock to reliably reproduce the test conditions.

6: Failure

Error reporting and handling has always been a challenge. Early solutions set global flags to indicate errors. These can be overwritten before the error condition is noticed. People also tried reporting errors by returning improbable *sentinel values* from a function. This requires programmers to know about those and to write code to analyze the return values. The biggest problem is psychological: programmers tend to be more interested in the successful scenario, where everything works right. It is too easy to forget or ignore error information.

6.1: Throwing Exceptions

Throwing exceptions to signal errors was a big step forward:

- Exceptions provide unified error reporting—there's only one way to do it.
- Exceptions cannot be ignored—they flow upward until caught or displayed on the console at program termination.
- Catching exceptions is the standardized way an operation can recover and retry.
- Exception hierarchies allow more general exception handlers to handle multiple exception subtypes.
- Errors are handled close to their origin or generalized by catching them "further out" so that multiple error sources are managed with a single handler.

Throwing exceptions was certainly an improvement over previous attempts to solve the error reporting problem. However, programmers eventually encountered pain points when scaling up to larger and more complex systems.

The main problem when throwing exceptions is that they are not tracked in the type system. A thrown exception is not a *result* of calling the function, but a Side Effect. You cannot know the exceptions you must handle when exception types are not part of the function signature. You can search the source code for explicitly thrown exceptions, but this manual process becomes harder as more functions are composed. Even then, built-in exceptions occur without evidence in the code. For example:

```
def divide(a: Int, b: Int): Int =
  a / b
```

The return type is simply `Int`, and there's no information about how `divide` might fail. `divide` looks like a pure function—but it actually throws `ArithmeticException` when `b` is zero. This example is trivial, but it demonstrates that failure information is not visible in the function signature and can easily be missed.

Suppose you handle all exceptions from a library—or at least, the exceptions you find in the documentation. Now a new version of that library comes out. You upgrade, assuming it must be better. Unbeknownst to you, the new version quietly throws a new type of exception. Because thrown exceptions are not shown in the function signature, the compiler cannot detect the change. Your code doesn't handle that exception. Your code was working. Nobody changed anything in your code. And yet it's broken. Worse, you only find out at runtime when the system fails.

Languages like C++ and Java tried to solve this problem by adding *exception specifications.* This notation adds exception types as part of the function's type signature. Unfortunately, exception specifications are a second, shadow type system. They are not managed using the same tools as the main type system. All attempts at using exception specifications failed. C++ abandoned exception specifications and checked exceptions in Java are now rarely used.

If error information is part of the type system, all possible errors are revealed by the type information. If a library component adds a new error, it must be reflected in the type signature. The type system immediately detects code that does not cover all error conditions.

6.2: The Functional Solution

The functional approach creates a package of information to return from the function. This package holds either the answer or error information. It is a new type that includes all possible failure types. Now the compiler has enough information to tell whether you've covered all failure possibilities.

Effects encapsulate the unpredictable parts of a system. Failure is unpredictable, so Effects must also express failure. How is success and failure information encoded into the function return type for an Effect System? This is what we've been doing with ZIO.succeed and ZIO.fail. The argument to succeed is the successful result value that you want to return. Calling succeed produces a type that says, "This Effect is OK." The argument to fail is the failure information. Calling fail produces a type that says, "Something went wrong in this Effect."

6.3: Failure Types

Although most examples in this book use a `String` argument for `fail`, you can use any type:

```
case object FailObject

class FailException extends Exception:
  override def toString: String =
    "FailException"

def failureTypes(n: Int) =
  n match
    case 0 =>
      ZIO.fail("String fail")
    case 1 =>
      ZIO.fail(FailObject)
    case _ =>
      ZIO.fail(FailException())
```

We use pattern matching to express the logic paths. `failureTypes` produces three different `fail` Effects:

- The `case 0` error type is a `String`, useful for this book's small code samples.
- The `case 1` error type is an object of type `FailObject`, demonstrating that any type works as failure information.
- The default case error type contains a `FailException` instance.

To make the code easier to read, we avoid function type signatures in this book and instead rely on type inference. The inferred type signature for `failureTypes` includes all three types: `String`, `FailObject` and `FailException`. The compiler uses that signature to verify that all error conditions are handled by any code that calls `failureTypes`.

Notice that `FailException` is never thrown. Placing an exception in a `fail` Effect returns the exception as a value. This is typically more information than a `String` provides, because the exception is a more specific type.

The `flip` operation takes a `ZIO.fail` and turns it into a `ZIO.succeed` so we can see the output instead of a stack trace. Here, we exercise all variations of `failureTypes`:

```
def run =
  defer:
    ZIO.debug("Begin failing").run
    failureTypes(0).flip.debug.run
    failureTypes(1).flip.debug.run
    failureTypes(2).flip.debug.run
    ZIO.debug("Done failing").run
```

Output:

```
Begin failing
String fail
FailObject
FailException
Done failing
```

Flipping the error and success conditions allows the whole sequence to run. Without `flip`, the first error terminates the `defer` block by *short-circuiting*.

6.4: Short-Circuiting

Short-circuiting is an important benefit of handling errors using an Effect System. When an Effect encounters an error, it prevents subsequent Effects from running unless the failure is handled. Like exceptions, an Effect System prevents further code from executing when an error occurs.

To demonstrate, `limitFail` fails if the value of n is greater than or equal to `limit`:

```
def limitFail(n: Int, limit: Int) =
  defer:
    ZIO.debug(s"Executing step $n").run
    if n < limit then
      ZIO.succeed(s"Completed step $n").run
    else
      ZIO.fail(s"Failed at step $n").run
```

We exercise `limitFail` with all its relevant argument values:

```
def shortCircuit(limit: Int) =
  defer:
    limitFail(0, limit).run
    limitFail(1, limit).run
    limitFail(2, limit).run
```

The debug shows short-circuiting behavior during failure:

```
def run =
  shortCircuit(0).flip
```

Output:

```
Executing step 0
Result: Failed at step 0
```

With `shortCircuit(0)`, the first step fails and the remainder of the `limitFail` calls do not happen. Without an Effect System, all the calls would be executed.

With `shortCircuit(1)`, the second step fails and the remainder of the `limitFail` calls do not happen:

```
def run =
  shortCircuit(1).flip
```

Output:

```
Executing step 0
Executing step 1
Result: Failed at step 1
```

With shortCircuit(2), the final step fails:

```
def run =
  shortCircuit(2).flip
```

Output:

```
Executing step 0
Executing step 1
Executing step 2
Result: Failed at step 2
```

With shortCircuit(3), there are no failures and all steps complete successfully:

```
def run =
  shortCircuit(3)
```

Output:

```
Executing step 0
Executing step 1
Executing step 2
Result: Completed step 2
```

This is one of the brilliant things about Effect Oriented error
handling. You don't write error-handling code when you call
a function that might produce an error. You write code for the
success path—you say what you want to happen. This code is
much easier to understand because the reader isn't constantly
wading through error-handling code.

6.5: Handling Failures

We will use these ideas in a temperature-measuring system.
Suppose an Effect `getTemperature` (implementation hidden)
can fail during a network request. All `getTemperature`
failures are returned as exceptions (returned, not thrown).
`getTemperature` doesn't fail when running in the `Success-
ful` scenario:

```
def run =
  Successful.simulate:
    getTemperature
```

Output:

```
Getting Temperature
Result: Temperature(35)
```

The `NetworkFailure` scenario introduces a simulated network problem. Now the program fails:

```
def run =
  NetworkFailure.simulate:
    getTemperature
```

Output:

```
Getting Temperature
Defect: NetworkException: Network Failure
```

Let's try to display something after attempting to get the
temperature. The unhandled failure causes short-circuiting
and the ZIO.debug never runs:

```
def run =
  NetworkFailure.simulate:
    defer:
      getTemperature.run
      ZIO.debug("succeeded").run
```

Output:

```
Getting Temperature
Defect: NetworkException: Network Failure
```

To make the debug run, we can capture the ZIO.fail containing the Exception and transform it into a ZIO.success:

```
val displayTemperature =
  getTemperature.catchAll:
    case e: Exception =>
      ZIO.succeed("getTemperature failed")

def run =
  NetworkFailure.simulate:
    defer:
      val result = displayTemperature.run
      ZIO.debug(result).run
```

Output:

```
Getting Temperature
getTemperature failed
```

The name `catchAll` is unfortunately confusing because it includes the word `catch`, implying that it is catching thrown exceptions. There are no thrown exceptions—`catchAll` is "catching" the typed errors produced by the Effect.

This time, `ZIO.debug` runs because we transform the `getTemperature` exception into a `ZIO.succeed`. However, succeeding with failure information is confusing.

Instead of capturing everything via the base `Exception` type, let's be more specific. We capture the `NetworkException` but this is not complete because it doesn't cover all failure possibilities:

```
val notExhaustive =
  getTemperature.catchAll:
    case ex: NetworkException =>
      ZIO.succeed:
        "Network Unavailable"
```

This results in a compiler warning:

```
warning:
match may not be exhaustive.
It would fail on pattern case: _: GpsException
```

To cover all possibilities we must also handle GpsException:

```
val temperatureAppComplete =
  getTemperature.catchAll:
    case ex: NetworkException =>
      ZIO.succeed:
        "Network Unavailable"
    case ex: GpsException =>
      ZIO.succeed:
        "GPS Hardware Failure"
```

Now the Effect completes successfully, despite the GPSFail-
ure scenario:

```
def run =
  GPSFailure.simulate:
    defer:
      val result = temperatureAppComplete.run
      ZIO.debug(result).run
```

Output:

```
Getting Temperature
GPS Hardware Failure
```

The new temperatureAppComplete has no failures. Trying
to catch failures from temperatureAppComplete produces a
compiler error:

```
val compilerError =
  temperatureAppComplete.catchAll:
    case ex: GpsException =>
      ZIO.succeed:
        "This cannot happen"
```

Output:

```
error:
This error handling operation assumes your
 effect can fail. However, your effect has
 no error type, which means it cannot fail
, so there is no need to handle failure.
```

The compiler reports that we included unusable code (for
conciseness, the error is truncated).

6.6: Multiple Failure Types

If an Effect produces multiple failure types, you must manage
all of them.

Consider a check Effect (implementation hidden) that fails
with a custom type ClimateFailure:

```
case class ClimateFailure(message: String)
```

```
def run =
  check(Temperature(-20))
```

Output:

```
Checking Temperature
Error: ClimateFailure(**Too Cold**)
```

The `weatherReportFaulty` Effect runs `getTemperature` followed by `check`:

```
val weatherReportFaulty =
  defer:
    val result = getTemperature.run
    check(result).run
```

`getTemperature` can produce `ZIO.fail` Effects containing `NetworkException` or `GpsException`, which are both `Exceptions`. `check` can produce a `ZIO.fail` containing `ClimateFailure`, which is not an `Exception`. To handle all failures for `weatherReportFaulty`, we provide a case for both `Exception` and `ClimateFailure`:

```
val weatherReport =
  weatherReportFaulty.catchAll:
    case exception: Exception =>
      ZIO.debug(exception.getMessage)
    case failure: ClimateFailure =>
      ZIO.debug(failure.message)
```

`getTemperature` produces two different `ZIO.fail` types. However, their contained failure objects are both `Exceptions`, so we can handle them both through `case exception`. You can also write a different `case` for each exception type.

When the combined Effect runs under the `TooCold` scenario, we get a `ClimateFailure`:

```
def run =
  TooCold.simulate:
    weatherReport
```

Output:

```
Getting Temperature
Checking Temperature
**Too Cold**
```

We don't see the `ClimateFailure` error, we only get its message as produced by the `catchAll`.

6.7: Handling Thrown Exceptions

So far, our example Effects *return* exceptions to indicate failure, but you might have legacy code or external libraries that *throw* exceptions instead. In these situations, we wrap exception-throwing code to return exceptions inside Effects, which is our preferred style.

`getTemperatureOrThrow` can fail by throwing an exception. If we call this function from an Effect, the program fails:

```
def run =
  NetworkFailure.simulate:
    ZIO.succeed:
      getTemperatureOrThrow()
```

Output:

```
Defect: NetworkException: Network Failure
```

Despite the claim made by ZIO.succeed that this Effect is successful, it crashes with a defect. The problem is Side-Effecting code—in this case, the thrown exception. When Side-Effecting code is involved, the Effect System cannot flag potential failures.

The solution is ZIO.attempt. This converts thrown Exceptions into Effects:

```
def safeTemperatureApp =
  ZIO.attempt:
    getTemperatureOrThrow()
```

Now you can use an Effect failure-handling mechanism like orElse:

```
def run =
  NetworkFailure.simulate:
    safeTemperatureApp.orElse:
      ZIO.succeed:
        "Could not get temperature"
```

Output:

```
Result: Could not get temperature
```

The Effect's failure is handled with a fallback, which succeeds.

Thrown exceptions are inherently unpredictable. We recommend encapsulating exception-throwing functions into Effects, which provide superior failure-handling mechanisms.

7: Composability

The essence of programming is *composition*: combining smaller pieces into larger pieces. Toy building bricks do not compose because of their colors or shapes or sizes. They compose because they have a generalized way to connect.

Composability basically means functions calling other functions. Although object-oriented systems *seem* different, those languages rearrange elements to turn them into ordinary function calls. Ultimately, functions are the foundation of all current languages.

Consider this basic composition example:

```
f(g(h()))
```

h produces a result that becomes the argument to g, and g's result becomes the argument to f. For this to work, the function result types must be *compatible* with the functions that consume those results.

This is where problems arise when attempting to compose functions. We want the simplicity of plugging together toy bricks, but we don't have their generalized interface. Instead, we have functions that produce incompatible result types, confounding our efforts to compose them with other functions.

Early Effect-like systems recognized this and made several attempts to generalize the interface between functions. Scala experiments began with the observation that many results could be converted into Futures. This worked in some cases, but Futures are not designed for this purpose and ultimately couldn't be usefully forced into the role.

A later approach uses *transformers.* A transformer converts a result into the type required by the next function call. This worked better but created a profusion of transformers for programmers to learn. Editing environments were unable to assist in transformer discovery via tab completion.

The approach in this book uses a generalized return type. This type is used throughout the Effect System, so every Effectful function returns this type. The type can be passed as an argument to other functions. A generalized return type solves the fundamental impediment to composition.

Issues that complicate composition include more than the return type. We must also handle:

- Failure
- Asynchronicity
- Resource management
- Cancellation
- Environmental requirements
- And more...

This chapter demonstrates problems with traditional composition and shows solutions using an Effect System. We illustrate with a progressive example that searches for news articles and summarizes them. We create a series of Effect parts, then compose those parts into the search application.

7.1: Composing with Effects

Basic functional programming attempted to solve the composition problem by providing types that hold results. Instead of directly returning a result, you return one of these types *containing* the result. Combining and converting these non-generalized types isn't too hard at first:

- An `Option` value can be converted to an `Either`.
- A `Try` can be converted to a `Future`.

However, it is sometimes impossible to convert types. Suddenly the problems become challenging and confusing:

- A `Future` cannot be converted to a `Try` without losing its asynchronous behavior.
- A managed resource type cannot also be an asynchronous type.
- A cancellable type cannot be represented as an `Either` type.
- A blocking type cannot also be a fallible type.

An Effect System with a universal type ergonomically represents all these concerns. This type is not truly universal, but it covers most concerns. It loses some semantics of the specialized types and provides many advantages in return.

Note: To maintain focus on composability, we use a number of predefined functions with hidden implementations. These implementations are included in the example code[1].

7.2: Future

We begin with Scala's typical asynchronous type:

---

[1]https://effectorientedprogramming.com/resources/zio/examples/2024-09-17

```
import scala.concurrent.Future
```

This has several unfortunate characteristics:

- It starts executing immediately.
- Cleanup is not guaranteed.
- It uses exceptions to report failures.
- Users must constantly pass `ExecutionContext` (the thread pool).

The first hidden-implementation function is `getHeadline`. It returns a `Future[String]`:

```
val future: Future[String] = getHeadline()
```

You cannot use a `Future` directly in an Effect System, but you can transform it into an `Effect` using `ZIO.from`. Doing so:

- Defers execution.
- Attaches finalizer behavior.
- Customizes the failure type.
- Gets the required `ExecutionContext`.

`getHeadlineZ` converts `getHeadline` into a ZIO Effect (the aforementioned "generalized return type"):

```
case class HeadlineNotAvailable()

val getHeadlineZ =
  ZIO
    .from:
      getHeadline()
    .orElseFail:
      HeadlineNotAvailable()
```

Because `ZIO.from(getHeadline())` produces a ZIO, we can add `orElseFail` to attach fallback behavior. If anything goes wrong, `orElseFail` produces a `ZIO.fail` containing `HeadlineNotAvailable`. Here we use the `Successful` scenario to retrieve the headline:

```
def run =
  Successful.simulate:
    getHeadlineZ
```

Output:

```
Network - Getting headline
Result: stock market rising!
```

In the `HeadlineError` scenario, `orElseFail` invokes the fallback:

```
def run =
  HeadlineError.simulate:
    getHeadlineZ
```

Output:

```
Network - Getting headline
Error: HeadlineNotAvailable()
```

7.3: Option

`Option` produces `None` to indicate that a value is not available, otherwise it returns a value of the specified type. For example, `Option[String]` yields either a `String` value or `None`.

`Option` does not deal with issues like asynchronicity or failure types. Execution is not deferred, and `Option` cannot interrupt the code producing the `Option` value.

`findTopicOfInterest` is our second hidden-implementation function. Given a headline, it looks for words or phrases within that headline. If it finds one, it returns that word or phrase, otherwise it returns `None`. Here, we apply it to "a boring headline":

```
val result: Option[String] =
  findTopicOfInterest:
    "a boring headline"
```

Using `ZIO.from`, let's create a better fallback strategy when the headline is not interesting. `ZIO.from` converts a missing value (`None`) into a generic failure. `orElseFail` produces a more descriptive type:

```
case class NoInterestingTopic(
    headline: String
)

def topicOfInterestZ(headline: String) =
  ZIO
    .from:
      findTopicOfInterest:
        headline
    .orElseFail:
      NoInterestingTopic(headline)
```

A headline containing "stock market" is considered interesting:

```
def run =
  topicOfInterestZ:
    "stock market rising!"
```

Output:

```
Analytics - Scanning for topic
Analytics - topic: Some(stock market)
Result: stock market
```

While "boring and inane" is uninteresting:

```
def run =
  topicOfInterestZ:
    "boring and inane"
```

Output:

```
Analytics - Scanning for topic
Analytics - topic: None
Error: NoInterestingTopic(boring and inane)
```

7.4: Either

Either holds objects of two different types specified in its type annotation. Like Option, execution is not deferred, and Either cannot interrupt the code producing the Either values.

wikiArticle is the third hidden-implementation function. It searches for articles on a topic—in this case, "stock market":

```
val wikiResult
    : Either[NoWikiArticle, String] =
  wikiArticle("stock market")
```

Note the similarity to Option. Instead of returning None, wikiArticle produces the descriptive type NoWikiArticle for failures.

ZIO.from converts wikiArticle into a ZIO:

```
def wikiArticleZ(topic: String) =
  ZIO.from:
    wikiArticle:
      topic
```

Now that it's a ZIO, we can plug it into the Effect System.

Searching for "stock market" produces an article:

```
def run =
  wikiArticleZ:
    "stock market"
```

Output:

```
Wiki - articleFor(stock market)
Result: detailed history of stock market
```

This is what failure looks like:

```
def run =
  wikiArticleZ:
    "barn"
```

Output:

```
Wiki - articleFor(barn)
Error: NoWikiArticle()
```

7.5: AutoCloseable

Java & Scala provide the `AutoCloseable` interface to define finalizer behavior for objects. This is an improvement over manual management, but static scoping limits its usability.

`openFile` is the fourth hidden-implementation function. It produces an `AutoCloseable`:

```
val file: AutoCloseable = openFile("file1")
```

We've been using ZIO.from to convert non-Effect-managing functions into Effectful ones. AutoCloseable, however, is a trait that can be implemented by arbitrary classes. ZIO.from cannot guess what an implementation might be or how to clean it up, so it cannot automatically manage the conversion. ZIO.fromAutoCloseable is specifically designed to deal with AutoCloseables. However, it only works with things that are already ZIOs. To solve this, we take the simplest approach by passing openFile to ZIO.succeed, producing a ZIO for fromAutoCloseable:

```
def openFileZ(path: String) =
  ZIO.fromAutoCloseable:
    ZIO.succeed:
      openFile(path)
```

Because we've applied fromAutoCloseable, the ZIO runtime manages the lifecycle of this object via the Scope mechanism. The file automatically closes when it is no longer used. For a more thorough discussion of Scope, see the ZIO documentation[2].

Let's see if a File contains a topic of interest. Conveniently, openFile has a contains method:

```
def run =
  defer:
    val file = openFileZ("file1").run
    file.contains:
      "topicOfInterest"
```

Output:

---

[2]https://effectorientedprogramming.com/resources/zio/docs

```
File - OPEN: file1
File - contains(topicOfInterest) => false
File - CLOSE: file1
Result: false
```

The file closes automatically, as we desire.

Standard Scala manages resources with Using:

```scala
import scala.util.Using

def run =
  defer:
    Using(openFile("file1")):
      file1 =>
        Using(openFile("file2")):
          file2 =>
            Using(openFile("file3")):
              file3 =>
                sameContents:
                  List(file1, file2, file3)
            .get
        .get
    .get
```

Output:

```
File - OPEN: file1
File - OPEN: file2
File - OPEN: file3
side-effect print: comparing content
File - CLOSE: file3
File - CLOSE: file2
File - CLOSE: file1
Result: true
```

Each additional file creates another level of code nesting.
Contrast this with:

```
def run =
  defer:
    val file1 = openFileZ("file1").run
    val file2 = openFileZ("file2").run
    val file3 = openFileZ("file3").run
    sameContents:
      List(file1, file2, file3)
```

Output:

```
File - OPEN: file1
File - OPEN: file2
File - OPEN: file3
side-effect print: comparing content
File - CLOSE: file3
File - CLOSE: file2
File - CLOSE: file1
Result: true
```

The Effect Oriented code remains flat. The automatic resource management is handled through the type system instead of being sprinkled throughout the code. This makes the
code easier to write and comprehend.

In this example, the file objects are created dynamically:

```
def run =
  defer:
    val fileNames =
      List("file1", "file2", "file3")

    val files =
      ZIO.foreach(fileNames)(openFileZ).run

    sameContents(files)
```

Output:

```
File - OPEN: file1
File - OPEN: file2
File - OPEN: file3
side-effect print: comparing content
File - CLOSE: file3
File - CLOSE: file2
File - CLOSE: file1
Result: true
```

Try-with-resources only works when all resource-managed
objects are available at compile time. ZIO's resource management works with dynamic values.

7.6: Try

`scala.util.Try` is similar to `Either` in that it returns one
of two types:

- An `Exception` if it fails.
- A result if it succeeds.

`write` is the fifth hidden-implementation function. It produces either a `Try` containing a `String` if it succeeds, or an
`Exception` if it fails. Note that it doesn't throw the exception:

```
val writeResult: Try[String] =
  openFile("file1").write("asdf")
```

We convert it to a ZIO using ZIO.from and change the
Exception into a FileWriteFailure:

```
case class FileWriteFailure()

def writeToFileZ(
    file: File,
    content: String,
) =
  ZIO
    .from:
      file.write:
        content
    .orElseFail:
      FileWriteFailure()
```

We write to a file without concerning ourselves with either
errors or resource cleanup:

```
def run =
  defer:
    val file = openFileZ("file1").run
    writeToFileZ(file, "New data").run
```

Output:

```
File - OPEN: file1
File - write: New data
File - CLOSE: file1
Result: New data
```

7.7: Exceptions

We previously covered the deficiencies of functions that throw exceptions. `summaryFor` is a hidden-implementation function that throws an exception when its argument is a particular search term. When successful, it produces a summary:

```
def run =
  defer:
    openFile("file1").summaryFor("space")
```

Output:

```
File - OPEN: file1
File - summaryFor(space)
Result: space is huge
```

With the wrong parameter, `summaryFor` throws an Exception:

```
def run =
  defer:
    openFile("file1").summaryFor("unicode")
```

Output:

```
File - OPEN: file1
File - summaryFor(unicode)
File - * Threw Exception *
Defect: FileSystem error
```

`ZIO.attempt` converts exception-throwing functions into Effects. `attempt` runs its argument and converts exceptions into `ZIO.fail` Effects. Here we attach an `orElseFail` that produces a descriptive type:

```
case class FileReadFailure(topic: String)

def summaryForZ(file: File, topic: String) =
  ZIO
    .attempt:
      file.summaryFor(topic)
    .orElseFail:
      FileReadFailure(topic)
```

Thus, any exception-throwing function is easily converted into a ZIO.

7.8: Slow Functions

Most examples in this chapter handle specific failure conditions. However, some functions are simply too slow. Latency is a cost of doing business, but it can become unacceptable.

The hidden-implementation function summarize uses a local *Large Language Model* (LLM). The performance of summarize varies wildly, and it has different failure modes compared to the other functions.

```
def run =
  defer:
    summarize("long article")
```

Output:

```
AI - summarize - start
AI - summarize - end
Result: short summary
```

summarize is a blocking function, which isn't obvious from the signature. This produces downsides:

- Concurrent blocking operations can prevent the progress of other operations.
- Blocking functions are difficult to manage.
- Blocking performance can vary significantly between environments.

ZIO uses a different model for interruption and cancellation, which is more accurate and reliable than the one used by the JVM. To convert `summarize` into a `ZIO` that doesn't block, we use `attemptBlockingInterrupt`. Then we can attach `ZIO` behaviors:

```
import java.util.concurrent.TimeoutException

def summarizeZ(article: String) =
  ZIO
    .attemptBlockingInterrupt:
      summarize(article)
    .onInterrupt:
      ZIO.debug("AI **INTERRUPTED**")
    .timeoutFail(TimeoutException()):
      4.seconds
```

If the ZIO is interrupted, the attached `onInterrupt` provides a handler. `timeoutFail` performs the interrupt, producing `TimeoutException` if `summarize` takes longer than four seconds. This confines the impact of `summarize` to `summarizeZ`.

For a reasonably sized article, `summarizeZ` does not time out:

```
def run =
  summarizeZ("long article")
```

Output:

```
AI - summarize - start
AI - summarize - end
Result: short summary
```

Long-running calls are interrupted if they take too long:

```
def run =
  summarizeZ("space")
```

Output:

```
AI - summarize - start
AI - taking a long time
AI **INTERRUPTED**
Error: java.util.concurrent.TimeoutException
```

`attemptBlockingInterrupt` is only for CPU-heavy tasks that can be forcibly killed without risk. It has a performance impact that must be considered when implementing an upper bound. It is not commonly used, so you'll typically rely on the other conversions in this chapter.

7.9: Composing an Application

You can compose Effects in any combination and sequence. `researchHeadline` combines the pieces created throughout this chapter.

We use type inference throughout the book, but `research-Headline` has explicit type annotations to emphasize that ordinary types are produced inside the `defer` block. All traces of Effects vanish once we call `.run` on them.

```
val researchHeadline =
  defer:
    val headline: String = getHeadlineZ.run

    val topic: String =
      topicOfInterestZ(headline).run

    val summaryFile: File =
      openFileZ("summaries").run

    if summaryFile.contains(topic) then
      summaryForZ(summaryFile, topic).run
    else
      val wikiArticle: String =
        wikiArticleZ(topic).run

      val summary: String =
        summarizeZ(wikiArticle).run

      writeToFileZ(summaryFile, summary).run

      summary
```

This application handles real-world situations that, without
Effects, require significantly more complicated code. It has
all the automation provided by Effects, but the code is still
clean and transparent to write and to understand.

We test researchHeadline against each scenario:

7.9.1: Headline Not Available

If it cannot get the current headline, researchHeadline fails
on the first step:

```
def run =
  HeadlineError.simulate:
    researchHeadline
```

Output:

```
Network - Getting headline
Error: HeadlineNotAvailable()
```

7.9.2: No Interesting Topic in Headline

In the BoringTopic scenario, the headline is uninteresting:

```
def run =
  BoringTopic.simulate:
    researchHeadline
```

Output:

```
Network - Getting headline
Analytics - Scanning for topic
Analytics - topic: None
Error: NoInterestingTopic(boring content)
```

7.9.3: Exception when Reading from File

We get a headline containing an interesting topic, but re-searchHeadline fails when checking if there's already a summary for that topic:

```
def run =
  FileSystemError.simulate:
    researchHeadline
```

Output:

```
Network - Getting headline
Analytics - Scanning for topic
Analytics - topic: Some(unicode)
File - OPEN: summaries
File - contains(unicode) => true
File - summaryFor(unicode)
File - * Threw Exception *
File - CLOSE: summaries
Error: FileReadFailure(unicode)
```

Even though `summaryFor` throws an exception, the file is closed properly and the error is clearly reported.

7.9.4: No Wiki Article Available

If we get through the previous steps and successfully read from the file, we can still fail when trying to get a wiki article:

```
def run =
  WikiSystemError.simulate:
    researchHeadline
```

Output:

```
Network - Getting headline
Analytics - Scanning for topic
Analytics - topic: Some(barn)
File - OPEN: summaries
File - contains(barn) => false
Wiki - articleFor(barn)
File - CLOSE: summaries
Error: NoWikiArticle()
```

7.9.5: AI Too Slow

Here we successfully get the wiki article, but the `AISlow`
scenario means the AI is too slow to summarize it:

```
def run =
  AISlow.simulate:
    researchHeadline
```

Output:

```
Network - Getting headline
Analytics - Scanning for topic
Analytics - topic: Some(space)
File - OPEN: summaries
File - contains(space) => false
Wiki - articleFor(space)
AI - summarize - start
AI - taking a long time
AI **INTERRUPTED**
File - CLOSE: summaries
Error: java.util.concurrent.TimeoutException
```

7.9.6: Disk Full

Next we have a headline, an interesting topic, a wiki article, and a summary. With the `DiskFull` scenario, we fail on the last step when trying to write the summary to the file:

```
def run =
  DiskFull.simulate:
    researchHeadline
```

Output:

```
Network - Getting headline
Analytics - Scanning for topic
Analytics - topic: Some(genome)
File - OPEN: summaries
File - contains(genome) => false
Wiki - articleFor(genome)
AI - summarize - start
AI - summarize - end
File - disk full!
File - CLOSE: summaries
Error: FileWriteFailure()
```

Despite this, the system is still in a consistent state. All resources are cleaned up properly.

7.9.7: Success

Finally, we make it through the gauntlet of failure possibilities and resource management, and complete a full `research-Headline` sequence:

```
def run =
  Successful.simulate:
    researchHeadline
```

Output:

```
Network - Getting headline
Analytics - Scanning for topic
Analytics - topic: Some(stock market)
File - OPEN: summaries
File - contains(stock market) => false
Wiki - articleFor(stock market)
AI - summarize - start
AI - summarize - end
File - write: market is moving
File - CLOSE: summaries
Result: market is moving
```

7.10: Effects are Values

Representing a complex workflow as a value allows manipulations that are impossible with non-Effect approaches. This can be difficult to remember when viewing and executing larger programs.

Suppose we get a new requirement that the process must complete within a strict time limit. Although we already have a timeout on the AI `summarize` call, we can still attach a more restrictive timeout to the entire `researchHeadline` function:

```
val quickResearch =
  researchHeadline
    .timeoutFail("strict timeout"):
      100.milliseconds


def run =
  Successful.simulate:
    quickResearch
```

Output:

```
Network - Getting headline
Analytics - Scanning for topic
Analytics - topic: Some(stock market)
File - OPEN: summaries
File - contains(stock market) => false
Wiki - articleFor(stock market)
File - CLOSE: summaries
Error: strict timeout
```

The timeout is exceeded before `quickResearch` completes.

We can repeatedly compose a program value with itself, spaced out by a delay. Here we create a single-shot workflow that analyzes the current headline every day:

```
val daily =
  Successful.simulate:
    quickResearch.repeat:
      Schedule.spaced(24.hours)
```

Imagine the work required to modify a system like this without using Effects.

8: Shared State

Immutable values provide many benefits but are impractical in some situations.

One approach constrains mutable values within code you know and control. You can write bug-free code if you're careful enough, but that code is fragile and easily broken by code changes.

This is particularly true when concurrency is involved—and concurrency is a core feature of Effect Systems. With concurrency, multiple different parts of your code can read and write shared state *at the same time.* The mutable value might be in an uncertain state when it is read, and multiple simultaneous writes to that value can produce incorrect results.

Effect Systems provide solutions for working with shared mutable state. This chapter demonstrates the need for those solutions and how to apply them.

Although concurrency drives the need to manage shared state, concurrency strategies are a complex topic, beyond the scope of this book. To focus on shared state, we use a hidden function called `parallel` that contains the concurrency portion of the examples.

8.1: Unreliable State

`parallel` takes an `Int` argument indicating the number of parallel Effects to run. In the following example, the Effect `increment` mutates the `var counter`. This seems innocent enough. And placing the mutation

```
counter = counter + 1
```

inside a ZIO should make it safe, right?

```
def run =
  val num       = 30_000
  var counter = 0
  val increment =
    ZIO.succeed:
      counter = counter + 1

  parallel(num):
    increment
  .as:
    s"Lost updates: ${num - counter}"
```

Output:

```
Result: Lost updates: 11
```

The as operation converts the success value of an Effect to the as argument, in this case the string we want to display.

The final value of `counter` should be num, but it appears to lose updates. With multiple instances of `increment` running in parallel, `counter = counter + 1` can get an incorrect value when reading `counter`. It can also update the value of `counter` at the same time as another instance of `increment`.

The final value of `counter` is unpredictable, so each time we regenerate this book we get a different result for the number of lost updates.

Unsafe mutability produces unpredictable results. Performing Side Effects inside a ZIO does not make them safe.

8.2: Reliable State

ZIO.Ref solves the problem of mutable values and concurrency by guarding the mutable value. Ref.make produces a new Ref Effect containing the given initialization value and its inferred type. Here, counter is a Ref containing an Int initialized to zero:

```
def increment(count: Ref[Int]) =
  count.update:
    value => value + 1

def run =
  defer:
    val counter = Ref.make(0).run
    parallel(30_000):
      increment(counter)
    .run
    s"counter: ${counter.get.run}"
```

Output:

```
Result: counter: 30000
```

increment calls update, a Ref method that accepts a function. update extracts the current value from the Ref and hands it to the function. The function produces a new value that update places back into the Ref. Here, the lambda value => value + 1 increments the value by one.

Because it is a Ref, any changes to counter are completely reliable. The final count is always correct. Updates happen using a non-blocking algorithm that we will explore further.

8.3: Effects Are Not Allowed

Ref seems like it should solve all our shared-state problems.
Let's try giving count.update a lambda that yields an Effect:

```
def increment(count: Ref[Int]) =
  count.update:
    value => ZIO.succeed(value + 1)
```

Output:

```
error:
Found:    ZIO
Required: Int
    value => ZIO.succeed(value + 1)
             ^^^^^^^^^^^^^^^^^^^^^^^
```

The type checker doesn't allow Effects here! When using a
Ref, you can only pass pure functions into update.

8.4: Sneaking in Side Effects

This is annoying, so let's try forcing our way to a solution.
We'll add a Side Effect in the form of attempts, an instance
of a class called AttemptCounter (implementation hidden).
Each call to increment also increments attempts. The function becomes impure because calling increment multiple
times with the same input leaves the system in a different
state each time. The Effect System, however, cannot tell that
modifying attempts is a Side Effect, so it lets us get away
with it:

```
val attempts = AttemptCounter()

def increment(count: Ref[Int]) =
  count.update:
    value =>
      attempts.increment
      value + 1

def run =
  defer:
    val counter = Ref.make(0).run
    parallel(30_000):
      increment(counter)
    .run

    s"""
      |counter: ${counter.get.run}
      |attempts: ${attempts.get}
      |""".stripMargin
```

Output:

```
Result:
counter: 30000
attempts: 30377
```

`AttemptCounter` uses Java's `AtomicInteger` to track attempts. Choosing an `AtomicInteger` as our Side Effect has a convenient benefit: it is immune to parallelism issues. attempts accurately counts every time we call `increment`. Although counter is 30,000 as desired, attempts is greater than 30,000. Somehow we called `increment` more than 30,000 times to produce a counter of 30,000.

It's not essential that you understand the non-blocking update mechanism explained in the next two paragraphs; you can skip them if you are not interested. They can be helpful if you want to imagine what is happening.

First, the value is read and stored. The stored value is then used to calculate the new value using our code—in this case, `value + 1`. But before the new value is placed back into the `Ref`, the current value in the `Ref` is compared to the stored value. If the `Ref` value is the same as the stored value, no other task has modified the `Ref` while the new value was calculated, so it is safe to store the new value into the `Ref`. To guarantee safe results, this *compare and swap* must be a single atomic operation, supported by either the hardware or the language.

If the `Ref` value is *not* the same as the stored value, it means some other task has modified the `Ref` in the meantime. Because of this *contention*, it is *not* safe to store the new value. The calculation is thrown away, and the whole process restarts by reading and storing the `Ref` value and performing the calculation again. These attempts repeat until there is no contention.

When using a pure function, repeated attempts are not a problem because pure functions have no Side Effects. We can try again and again without harming our system. An Effect is a different matter because an Effect can only be performed once. This is why the Effect System prevents us from using

```
value => ZIO.succeed(value + 1)
```

to update the `Ref`, because contentions re-execute the Effect. The Effect System keeps us from making mistakes.

8.5: Reliable Effects

To prevent Effect retries while updating a Ref, use a variation called Ref.Synchronized. This uses a lock that must first be acquired by any task attempting to update the Ref. When one task holds the lock, no other tasks are able to access the Ref until the first task completes and then releases the lock. This guarantees only a single execution of the update body, including its contained Effects. By replacing Ref.make with Ref.Synchronized.make, each Effect is only executed once:

```
val attempts = AttemptCounter()

def increment(count: Ref.Synchronized[Int]) =
  count.updateZIO:
    value =>
      ZIO.succeed:
        attempts.increment
        value + 1

def run =
  defer:
    val counter =
      Ref.Synchronized.make(0).run
    parallel(30_000):
      increment(counter)
    .run

    s"""
       |counter: ${counter.get.run}
       |attempts: ${attempts.get}
       |""".stripMargin
```

Output:

```
Result:
counter: 30000
attempts: 30000
```

In the previous example, `count.update` takes a pure function. Here, `count.updateZIO` takes a function that produces a `ZIO`.

The output shows that each Effect executes only once. The lock-free algorithm is used for pure functions because it is typically faster. Here, we must use locking because accidentally retrying Effects will change the behavior of the application.

9: Resilience

A resilient system behaves predictably during high loads or hostile situations. If failures occur, the system either recovers or shuts down in a well-defined manner.

Effects are the parts of a system that are unpredictable. The goal of resilience when applied to Effects is to mitigate these unpredictabilities.

Consider a request to a remote service. You cannot know if the network is working or if that service is available. Perhaps the service is under a heavy load and slow to respond.

Effect Systems provide strategies to compensate for those issues without invasive restructuring. For example, one approach to a poorly responding server is to attach fallback behavior. If a request to a preferred service doesn't produce a response quickly enough, you can make a request to a secondary service.

Traditional coding requires extensive re-architecting to apply and adapt resilience strategies. With Effects, resilience strategies are easily incorporated and modified. This chapter demonstrates some approaches and supporting components that enhance program resilience.

9.1: Caching

Caching is a strategy for mitigating resilience issues. The first time you make a new request to a service, the cache stores the result. If you make an identical request, that result is immediately returned and the service is not called.

A cache compensates for services that are:

- Slow: A cache speeds response time.
- Brittle: A cache provides stable responses and minimizes the risk of overwhelming the resource.
- Expensive: A cache reduces calls to the service, lowering operating cost.

To test cache resilience, consider one worst-case scenario a service might encounter: the *Thundering Herd.* This is a common problem in networked environments. It occurs when a system receives a large set of simultaneous requests, all asking for the same data. Naive caching does not recognize that only one request should be made to the underlying service. It allows many requests through before the first request completes and is stored in the cache. The initial response is not available to serve the duplicate requests, wasting CPU resources and slowing response time. It also stresses the underlying service that we want to protect.

Here, `thunderingHerds` is an Effect that uses a `PopularService` (implementation hidden) to simultaneously retrieve 100 identical requests:

```
val thunderingHerds =
  defer:
    val popularService =
      ZIO.service[PopularService].run

    val memes =
      List.fill(100):
        popularService.retrieve:
          "Awesome Memes"

    ZIO.collectAllPar(memes).run

    ZIO
      .serviceWithZIO[CloudStorage]:
        storage => storage.invoice
      .run
```

memes is a List filled via Effects that all retrieve "Awesome Memes". We use List.fill rather than repeatN because repeatN is sequential. List.fill creates a collection of requests that can be executed sequentially or in parallel.

Calling collectAllPar causes each of these requests to start in parallel, so all the identical requests arrive at popularService simultaneously.

popularService uses CloudStorage, which keeps track of the requests for billing purposes. CloudStorage.invoice tells us how much we've spent.

Now we define makePopularService so it uses the CloudStorage service without caching. To construct a PopularService, we provide the Effect that looks up content. In this case, it uses storage.retrieve:

```
val makePopularService =
  defer:
    val storage =
      ZIO.service[CloudStorage].run

    PopularService(storage.retrieve)
```

Running thunderingHerds with the un-cached PopularService demonstrates the problem:

```
def run =
  thunderingHerds.provide(
    CloudStorage.live,
    ZLayer.fromZIO(makePopularService),
  )
```

Output:

```
Result: Amount owed: $100
```

Each request to CloudStorage costs one dollar. The invoice is 100 dollars because all 100 requests reach our CloudStorage provider, even though 99 of them are redundant.

We improve the situation by constructing a PopularService with a cache from the zio-cache[1] library:

---

[1]https://effectorientedprogramming.com/resources/zio/zio-cache

```
import zio.cache.Cache

val makeCachedPopularService =
  defer:
    val storage =
      ZIO.service[CloudStorage].run

    val cache =
      Cache
        .make(
          capacity = 1,
          timeToLive = Duration.Infinity,
          lookup = Lookup(storage.retrieve),
        )
        .run

    PopularService(cache.get)
```

The basic Cache is created using make. The capacity
argument sets the size of the cache. Here, we make it tiny
since we are only caching a single result.

The timeToLive argument tells the cache how long to hold
its results. A Duration of Infinity means the cache never
throws away its results. Because the cache is in memory and
not in persistent storage, the cache holds its results until the
application is terminated.

The lookup argument is created by handing the
retrieval Effect to the Lookup constructor. Handing it
storage.retrieve wraps the new cache around the
storage service. Now when we create the PopularService
using cache.get, the cache receives the requests first and
decides which requests proceed to CloudStorage.

We repeat the previous example, replacing
makePopularService with makeCachedPopularService:

```
def run =
  thunderingHerds.provide(
    CloudStorage.live,
    ZLayer.fromZIO:
      makeCachedPopularService,
  )
```

Output:

```
Result: Amount owed: $1
```

The invoice is now one dollar, because only the first of the
redundant requests reaches the `CloudStorage` provider. We
still perform the same 100 requests in parallel and use the
same cloud storage, but we return the cached result for the
redundant 99 requests. The result of the first request is
successfully stored and then retrieved for the remaining requests, even though all requests arrived simultaneously. The
cache automatically watches for redundant requests arriving
at the same time and only passes the first one through for
processing. Once that finishes, the result goes into the cache
and the remaining redundant requests are served from the
cache.

Savings are rarely this extreme, but it is reassuring to know
we can easily handle such situations.

9.2: Rate Limits

NOTE: The next three sections use the `rezilience` library[2],
an open-source package that not part of the standard ZIO

---

[2]https://www.vroste.nl/rezilience/docs/

library. `rezilience` is a small collection of data types that make asynchronous systems more resilient to failure.

Rate limits create agreements between services. If you exceed the limit, you can crash the underlying service or be charged expensive penalties.

`expensiveCall` is an hidden-implementation Effect representing a call to a delicate service. A business contract specifies that we only perform `expensiveCall` once every second.

Here, we do *not* respect the contract:

```
def run =
  defer:
    val startTime = Clock.instant.run
    expensiveCall(startTime, "User")
      .repeatN(2)
      .run
```

Output:

```
User request @ 0s
User request @ 0s
User request @ 0s
```

To demonstrate the behavior of the system, `expensiveCall` takes the `startTime` produced by the `Clock` and the identity of the caller.

`repeatN` executes as quickly as possible, with no throttling between calls. The three requests arrive on top of each other, without pause. There's no respect for the rate limit.

A *rate limiter* forces requests to be spread out in time so they don't arrive too quickly and overwhelm a service. To define

a `RateLimiter`, `max` is the number of requests allowed per
interval. Here, the `RateLimiter` allows one per second:

```
import nl.vroste.rezilience.RateLimiter

val makeRateLimiter =
  RateLimiter
    .make(max = 1, interval = 1.second)
```

9.2.1: Single-Case Limiting

We wrap the unrestricted `expensiveCall` Effect inside our
`RateLimiter`:

```
def run =
  defer:
    val startTime   = Clock.instant.run
    val rateLimiter = makeRateLimiter.run
    rateLimiter:
      expensiveCall(startTime, "User")
    .repeatN(2)
      .run
```

Output:

```
User request @ 0s
User request @ 1s
User request @ 2s
```

Even though `repeatN` still attempts to send all three requests
as quickly as it can, `rateLimiter` slows down the execution
of these requests. The first request goes through immediately,
and each later request is delayed by one second. Now the
system adheres to our service agreement.

9.2.2: Application-Wide Limiting

The same `RateLimiter` can be used across an application. This allows an arbitrary number of users and modules to access the service, while ensuring that the application as a whole respects the rate limit. Each additional user gets a smaller fraction of the rate limit:

$$userRate = rateLimit/numberOfUsers$$

This means:

```
1 user makes 1 request per second
2 users each make 1 request every 2 seconds
3 users each make 1 request every 3 seconds
```

To test this, we create three parallel users that each submit requests as fast as they can. `foreachPar` executes an Effect for each element of a collection. Here it takes each element of `users` and passes it as `user` to its lambda, which runs our rate-limited logic. `foreachPar` returns a collection of results, which we do not care about in this case. We use `.as` to provide a single result message instead.

```
def run =
  defer:
    val rateLimiter = makeRateLimiter.run
    val users =
      List("Bill ", "Bruce", "James")
    val startTime = Clock.instant.run
    ZIO
      .foreachPar(users):
        user =>
          rateLimiter:
            expensiveCall(startTime, user)
          .repeatN(2)
```

```
    .as("All requests succeeded")
    .run
```

Output:

```
Bill  request @ 0s
James request @ 1s
Bruce request @ 2s
Bill  request @ 3s
James request @ 4s
Bruce request @ 5s
Bill  request @ 6s
James request @ 7s
Bruce request @ 8s
Result: All requests succeeded
```

The rate limiter is applied globally across the parallel effects. The first request goes through immediately. Each subsequent request is delayed by one second, regardless of where the request originates. The power of this guarantee grows with the complexity of the system.

9.3: Constraining Concurrent Requests

A rate limiter is one way to prevent a system from accidentally overwhelming a service. It limits us to a certain number of requests per unit of time. Some services limit the number of requests they can receive simultaneously. This produces a different way to overwhelm the service.

A *bulkhead* constrains the number of requests that can pass through at once. The bulkheads in a submarine are small doors that separate sections of the craft to prevent problems like flooding or fires from destroying the entire submarine. Bulkheads restrict the passage of sailors through a door at the same time. Any sailors that cannot pass through queue up to wait their turn.

The software `Bulkhead` does the same thing by limiting the number of concurrent requests and queueing excess requests for eventual processing.

In this example, a `DelicateResource` can only accept three simultaneous requests. More than that and it crashes:

```
def run =
  defer:
    val delicateResource =
      ZIO.service[DelicateResource].run
    ZIO
      .foreachPar(1 to 10):
        _ => delicateResource.request
      .as("All Requests Succeeded!")
      .run
  .provide(DelicateResource.live)
```

Output:

```
Delicate Resource constructed.
Do not make more than 3 concurrent requests!
Current requests: List(A)
Current requests: List(A, B)
Current requests: List(A, B, C)
Current requests: List(A, B, C, D)
Error: Crashed the server!!
```

Ten requests in parallel causes `delicateResource` to experience more than its restricted number of three.

We create a `Bulkhead` by giving it `maxInFlightCalls`. This determines the number of requests that can pass through simultaneously:

```scala
import nl.vroste.rezilience.Bulkhead

val makeBulkhead =
  Bulkhead.make(maxInFlightCalls = 3)
```

We wrap the original `delicateResource.request` in this `Bulkhead`:

```scala
def run =
  ZIO
    .scoped:
      defer:
        val bulkhead = makeBulkhead.run
        val delicateResource =
          ZIO.service[DelicateResource].run
        ZIO
          .foreachPar(1 to 10):
            _ =>
              bulkhead:
                delicateResource.request
          .as("All Requests Succeeded")
          .run
    .provide(DelicateResource.live)
```

Output:

```
Delicate Resource constructed.
Do not make more than 3 concurrent requests!
Current requests: List(A)
Current requests: List(A, B)
Current requests: List(A, B, C)
Current requests: List(B, C, D)
Current requests: List(C, D, E)
Current requests: List(D, E, F)
Current requests: List(E, F, G)
Current requests: List(F, G, H)
Current requests: List(G, H, I)
Current requests: List(H, I, J)
Result: All Requests Succeeded
```

The `Bulkhead` limits the number of simultaneous requests and the server does not crash.

Note the `Bulkhead` argument name `maxInFlightCalls`. This tells you that the `Bulkhead` is constraining the number of requests *that are currently being serviced.* Before more requests are accepted, one or more previous requests must complete, making the server available for more work.

9.4: Circuit Breaking

When a request fails, it is reasonable to immediately retry that request. However, unrestricted aggressive retries can compound the problem by increasing the load on a struggling service.

A `Schedule` is an Effect that defines a recurring schedule. Here, `rapidly` produces 140 repetitions, one every 50 milliseconds:

```
val rapidly =
  Schedule.recurs(140) &&
    Schedule.spaced(50.millis)
```

When unrestrained, all requests pass through to the degraded
externalService:

```
def run =
  defer:
    val callsMade = Ref.make(0).run
    val failures  = Ref.make(0).run
    externalService(callsMade, failures)
      .ignore
      .repeat(rapidly)
      .run

    val made   = callsMade.get.run
    val failed = failures.get.run

    s"""
      |Total Submitted: $made
      |Failed: $failed
      |""".stripMargin
```

Output:

```
Result:
Total Submitted: 141
Failed: 81
```

callsMade tracks the number of calls made to externalService. Using ignore means we don't care whether the result
of each request is a success or a failure—we just want to keep
firing requests at externalService.

In the `Result`, we see 141 requests because the `repeat` is in addition to the original call. This is too many requests and further degrades the `externalService`.

A `CircuitBreaker` tracks the number of failures. When there are too many failures, the `CircuitBreaker` blocks additional requests while the service recovers. While it is blocking requests, additional calls fail immediately with a `CircuitBreakerOpen` error.

Like a knife switch on an old-time electrical circuit breaker, when the switch is closed, the electric current (requests) passes through. When the switch is open, no electric current can flow (i.e., no requests can pass through).

After some time has elapsed (determined by the `resetPolicy` argument), the `CircuitBreaker` changes into "half-open" mode, when it allows one request to pass through. If that request succeeds, the circuit breaker goes back into the "closed" state and all requests pass through. If the request fails, it goes back to "open," waiting again until `resetPolicy` tells it to allow another excperiment.

This way, when a service begins to falter, the `Circuit-Breaker` gives it time to recover and then keeps testing to see when it *has* recovered.

The `trippingStrategy` argument for creating a `Circuit-Breaker` determines what "too many failures" means. There are two strategies:

- `failureCount` trips the breaker when the number of consecutive failures exceeds the given value. The following example uses this approach.
- `failureRate` trips the breaker when the proportion of failing calls to successful calls exceeds a threshold.

Here, we create a `CircuitBreaker` that changes to the "open" state when it counts two failures:

```
import nl.vroste.rezilience.{
  CircuitBreaker,
  TrippingStrategy,
  Retry,
}
import TrippingStrategy.failureCount

val circuitBreakerZ =
  CircuitBreaker.make(
    trippingStrategy = failureCount(2),
    resetPolicy = Retry.Schedules.common(),
  )
```

We use `Retry.Schedules.common()` to produce a typical `resetPolicy`. You can also specify a policy for *exponential backoff* or customize a policy using various different parameters:

- Minimum duration
- Maximum duration
- Factor for delay increase
- Whether to retry immediately
- Maximum number of retries
- Jitter factor

As before, we wrap the original Effect in the `Circuit-Breaker`. To watch the `CircuitBreaker` work, we track the number of calls successfully made versus calls that are prevented:

```scala
import CircuitBreaker.CircuitBreakerOpen

def run =
  defer:
    val circuitBreaker = circuitBreakerZ.run
    val callsMade      = Ref.make[Int](0).run
    val callsPrevented = Ref.make[Int](0).run
    val failures       = Ref.make[Int](0).run

    val protectedCall =
      circuitBreaker:
        externalService(callsMade, failures)
      .catchSome:
        case CircuitBreakerOpen =>
          callsPrevented.update(_ + 1)
        case other =>
          ZIO.unit

    protectedCall.ignore.repeat(rapidly).run

    val prevented = callsPrevented.get.run
    val made      = callsMade.get.run
    val failed    = failures.get.run
    s"""
       |Total Submitted: $made
       |Failed: $failed
       |Prevented: $prevented
       |""".stripMargin
```

Output:

```
Result:
Total Submitted: 67
Failed: 0
Prevented: 74
```

The circuit breaker prevents the majority of doomed calls
from passing through to the external service.

9.5: Reducing Worst-Case Latency

When making calls across complex, unpredictable networks, you can get very different response times between one call and the next. Some response times might be so long that your application won't meet its requirements.

Suppose we need a response time of just over a second, but our calculations use a service `intermittentSlowResponse` (implementation hidden) that occasionally takes significantly longer than a second:

```
def run =
  defer:
    val numFailed =
      lotsOfRequests(
        50_000,
        1.second,
        intermittentSlowResponse,
      ).run
    s"$numFailed requests timed out"
```

Output:

```
Result: 46 requests timed out
```

Many times, `intermittentSlowResponse` fails to meet our needs.

If the first call takes a long time, you can make a second, identical call (perhaps to a different server) and hope it returns more quickly. The second call might finish first, but the original call might finish first. We want to speed things up by taking the result that comes back sooner. To do this, we race the two requests against each other.

Hedging is a reference to financial investing, where you make a second investment to compensate for the potential losses of a first investment. When working with services, a hedging strategy sends a request, then waits a bit before sending a subsequent request. It takes the first result that arrives and cancels the other request. A hedging algorithm works like this:

- Determine the average response time for the fastest 50% of requests.
- If a call doesn't get a response within this duration, make an additional, identical request.
- Race the requests, returning the first successful response and cancelling the slower one.

This way, we recognize potentially slow responses and attempt to get faster results with a second call. The cost is a minor increase in the total requests made. It's not perfect and there are probabilities involved:

- Ordinarily, you have a $1/n$ chance of getting the worst case response time.
- Hedging produces a $1/n^2$ chance.
- If this doesn't eliminate the slowest responses, re-apply the same technique. This produces a $1/n^3$ chance of getting the worst performance.

A hedged Effect can be created using ZIO's `race` and `delay`. We begin by calling `intermittentSlowResponse`, which starts right away. We add a `race` against a second `intermittentSlowResponse` call. However, we don't want that second call to run immediately:

```
val hedged =
  intermittentSlowResponse.race:
    intermittentSlowResponse.delay:
      20.millis
```

Twenty milliseconds represents the response time for the
fastest 50% of our requests. The second call to `intermit-
tentSlowResponse` won't begin until the `delay` times out. If
the first call finishes before then, it wins the `race` before the
second call begins, so we never make the second call before
`race` cancels the Effect. If the first call doesn't finish before
the `delay` times out, the second call begins and the `race` is
on. Once there's a winner, `race` cancels the loser.

Hedging ensures we only make the second, potentially waste-
ful, call to `intermittentSlowResponse` when the first call
starts taking a suspiciously long time, which only happens
occasionally. The naive (non-hedged) approach always creates two requests and races them. That doubles the calls
to `intermittentSlowResponse` and probably makes things
worse.

Our hedged solution produces much better results:

```
def run =
  defer:
    val numFailed =
      lotsOfRequests(
        50_000,
        1.second,
        hedged,
      ).run

    s"$numFailed requests timed out"
```

Output:

```
Result: 0 requests timed out
```

Hedging the application meets its requirements.

9.6: Test Resilience

ZIO Test includes `TestAspects` that attach capabilities or restrictions to tests in a clean and focused way.

Of the several pre-made `TestAspects`, we highlight the two we find most useful. You can also make your own, attaching capabilities and restrictions that are pertinent to your domain.

9.6.1: Test Timeouts

If you have *service level agreements* (SLAs), tests help guarantee you meet those SLAs. Even if you don't have contracts, there are still good reasons to ensure that tests complete in a timely manner. Services like GitHub Actions automatically cancel a build if it takes too long. This only happens at a very coarse level—it only kills the job and doesn't show you the responsible test.

A common solution is to define a base test class for your project that all tests extend. In this class, you set a default upper limit on test duration. When a test violates this limit, it fails with a useful message. This helps identify tests that either lock up or take an unreasonable amount of time to complete.

For example, if you run tests in a *continuous integration and continuous delivery* (CI/CD) pipeline, you want those tests to complete quickly and produce rapid feedback. To attach a `TestAspect`, use `@@`. These can be chained:

```
def spec =
  test("long testZ"):
    defer:
      ZIO.sleep(1.hour).run
      assertCompletes
  @@ TestAspect.withLiveClock
    @@ TestAspect.timeout(1.second)
```

Output:

```
- long testZ
Timeout of 1 s exceeded.
```

Test results starting with a - are failures, and those starting
with a + are successes.

The default `TestClock` controls timing during ZIO tests.
A `TestClock` doesn't move forward on its own—the pro-
grammer must move it explicitly. This way, tests involv-
ing time can run much more quickly. Sometimes, however, we need the `TestClock` to run using the real time.
`TestAspect.withLiveClock` runs the test with `TestClock`
attached to a "live" clock.

`TestAspect.timeout` ensures that tests complete within a
given time.

9.6.2: Flaky Tests

As a project grows, tests can become unreliable. We call such
tests *flaky*. There are a number of contributing factors:

- Code using shared, live services. Other processes, such
  as a database or a file system, might alter these shared
  resources. These might be other tests in the project or
  even unrelated processes running on the same machine.

- Code that is not thread-safe—other processes might alter the expected state of the system.
- Resource limitations. A team of engineers might successfully run the test suite on their personal machines. However, the CI/CD system might not have enough resources to run the tests triggered by everyone pushing to the repository. Tests might also fail due to timeouts or lack of memory.

Because it uses `spottyLogic` (implementation hidden), this test is vulnerable to sporadic failures:

```
import zio.test.{assertTrue, test}

val troublesomeTestCase =
  test("flaky test!"):
    defer:
      val wasSuccessful = spottyLogic.run
      assertTrue(wasSuccessful)



def spec =
  troublesomeTestCase
```

Output:

```
Failed!
- flaky test!
  ☐ Result was false
  wasSuccessful
```

To fix this, we need only attach `TestAspect.flaky`:

```
def spec =
  troublesomeTestCase @@ TestAspect.flaky
```

Output:

```
Failed!
Failed!
Success!
+ flaky test!
```

With `TestAspect.flaky`, the test is repeated until it succeeds.

9.7: The Ecosystem of Effects

In this chapter, you've seen Effects combined to form powerful techniques for improving program resilience. This is only a glimpse of the things you can do with Effects. Effects provide a foundation to create more reliable, adaptable, and testable systems.

There are a number of libraries that build on these primitives and bring these benefits to other domains. The ZIO ecosystem contains libraries for stream processing, HTTP clients/servers, workflows, databases, event systems like Kafka, and many others. Check out the ZIO Reference[3] for core libraries. For the complete list of additional ways to use Effects, look at the ZIO Ecosystem[4].

---

[3]https://effectorientedprogramming.com/resources/zio/docs
[4]https://effectorientedprogramming.com/resources/zio/ecosystem

Index

www.ingramcontent.com/pod-product-compliance
Lightning Source LLC
Chambersburg PA
CBHW052032150726
48002CB00002B/558